SABIAN SYMBOLS IN CARD READING

THE SABIAN SYMBOLS
IN
CARD READING

Delle Fowler

SABIAN SYMBOLS
IN
CARD READING

A
MANUAL
FOR
READING
PLAYING CARDS
FOR
HIGHER GUIDANCE

BY

DELLE FOWLER

©2000 by Delle Fowler

No part of this publication may be reproduced or distributed in any form or by any means including but not limited to electronic, mechanical, photocopying, recording, or otherwise, or stored in a database or retrieval system, or transmitted in any form, except for the inclusion of brief quotations in a review, without prior permission in writing from the author.

The author may be contacted through the publisher.

Information on the Sabian Assembly may be obtained from the author or through the Sabian Assembly web site at http://www.sabian.org

Cover photograph by Delle Fowler
Cover design by David Fowler

Printed in Victoria, Canada

Canadian Cataloguing in Publication Data

Fowler, Delle, 1926-
  Sabian symbols in card reading

  ISBN 1-55212-420-7

  1. Fortune-telling by cards. 2. Astrology. 3. Self-realization--Miscellanea. I. Title.
  BF1879.A7F68 2000   133.3'242   C00-910874-2

TRAFFORD

Suite 6E, 2333 Government St., Victoria, B.C. V8T 4P4, CANADA
Phone   250-383-6864   Toll-free   1-888-232-4444 (Canada & US)
Fax   250-383-6804   E-mail   sales@trafford.com
Web site   www.trafford.com   TRAFFORD PUBLISHING IS A DIVISION OF TRAFFORD HOLDINGS LTD.
Trafford Catalogue #00-0085   www.trafford.com/robots/00-0085.html

10   9   8   7   6   5   4   3   2

TABLE OF CONTENTS

PROLOGUE ---ix

SABIAN SYMBOLS N CARD READING --1

USING CARDS FOR DIVINATION ---------------------------------10

THE LAYOUT OR ARCANUM ------------------------------------13

THE SEVEN LEVELS OF INTERPRETATION --------------------17

LAYING OUT THE ARCANUM ----------------------------------21

    FIGURE 1 ---24
    FIGURE 2 ---26

HOW TO READ THE ARCANUM ---------------------------------30

THE SUITS ---32

INTERPRETATION OF THE CARDS-----------------------------34

INDIVIDUAL KEYNOTE ---------------------------------------36

EXAMPLE LAYOUT --38

    DIAGRAM --39
    INTERPRETATION-----------------------------------40

THE FOUR WORLDS --43

    FIGURE 3 ---44

THE JOKER --51

THE CARDS
    DIAMONDS BEGIN ----------------------------------56
    SPADES BEGIN -------------------------------------82
    HEARTS BEGIN -------------------------------------108
    CLUBS BEGIN --------------------------------------134

EPILOGUE ---160

WORKSHEET *(FEEL FREE TO COPY)* ------------------------162

PROLOGUE

For all of you who are familiar with *The Sabian Symbols in Astrology* by Dr. Marc Edmund Jones there is a bit of explanation needed here in regard to the title of this book.

In 1925, in cooperation with Elsie Wheeler, Dr. Jones developed the Sabian Symbols that have long been used and appreciated by astrologers all over the world. Those are the symbols that are defined in *The Sabian Symbols in Astrology* for each of the 360 degrees of the zodiac. Before that, in 1923, Dr. Jones developed another set of Sabian Symbols in cooperation with Zoe Wells. This first set of symbols was assigned, one each, to the 52 playing cards of a regular card deck for divination purposes. These are the Sabian Symbols that this book speaks about.

The playing card symbols were incorporated into the inner discipline of the Sabian Assembly as a part of the Tarot work included there. This Tarot work is sacrosanct to Acolytes and Legates of the Sabian Assembly. When public interest in these symbols was expressed some years ago to several of the students in the Sabian Assembly, Dr. Jones requested that this Tarot, as he had gained it from a man named Sampson, not be taught or disseminated. He said this man had not wished it to be made public. There was, however, one big exception. Dr. Jones said that the keywords could be used, since they were his contribution along with Zoe Wells, and he gave his permission for these to be shared with the public.

As with the astrological symbols, each of the fifty-two cards is associated with an image or little picture. Unlike the astrological symbols, which have one keyword for each symbol, each card has a series of seven keywords associated with it. One of these keyword series is associated with each of the Sabian Tarot images (the symbols). Each keyword is also associated with one of seven different levels of consciousness. Dr. Jones stated that the psychic connection that was involved in his work with Zoe Wells was a part of a "strange genetic tie of some sort back into exceptionally early Mesopotamian or even earlier foundations of human intelligence." At that time he wasn't as concerned with this information and much that was obtained eventually slipped away. When he started working with the astrological symbols, he mentioned that the playing card symbols were too generalized or not specific enough.

Now that is the end of the story so far as Dr. Jones and Zoe Wells were concerned, but many years later, as I studied their work and spent endless hours working with this system of card reading, I became intensely interested in these symbols and the keywords. As the years went by and my expertise with the use of the cards developed and improved, it seemed to me that there was a connection between each of the levels and its keyword that hadn't been defined in the sparse notes that Dr. Jones and Zoe Wells left with us. I was beginning to sense that a deeper and more detailed scenario was involved with each of the symbolic pictures that accompanied each card. I started this work with the cards in October of 1972 and have literally worked with them almost every day since that time.

On June 13, 1997, I had an inexplicable urge to sit down at the computer and write about the cards. Specifically, the eight of Hearts was the first focus that started all of this that day. I've been psychic since my early childhood and over the past thirty-some years I have been working with what Dr. Jones referred to as "intellectual psychism," (a keenly developed sensitivity used against a background of experience and knowledge) as a part of the work within the Sabian Assembly. As I sat at the computer, the words flowed easily and naturally and the little word picture that had been given for this card was expanded into greater detail and specificity. Then each of the keywords, one for each level, was described in an orderly and comprehensive fashion. After I finished, I read over this material and was more than excited. What I had discovered was the integrated unification of the seven levels with the symbolic degree reading that I had always sensed could be discerned. Here it was! As I turned back to the computer, eager to continue, I was impressed with the idea that I should do one card each day until they were finished. I was to start in the morning and do only one card a day. This procedure was followed until each of the fifty-two cards had been described. I also added a comment on the Joker.

At the end of the work on that first day I had a fleeting glimpse of a seal or an insignia of some kind. It was embossed, and the design was highly stylized and three dimensional. I was not paying very much attention to it and, then, suddenly, I realized I had to do my best to keep it in memory as I recalled Marc saying that Zoe Wells had also been given a seal that she unfortunately didn't retain. Was this the same insignia? As I mention in the section on the Jack of Spades, page 103, in this book, I really cannot know, but it appears to be significantly connected to the early Mesopotamian source that Dr. Jones mentioned in respect to this work in general and especially when that card is involved in an individual layout.

Delle Fowler
October 28, 1998

West Palm Beach, FL

The Sabian Assembly is an arcane discipline and fellowship working with the new cabala, philosophy and Bible lessons. For those interested, a person-centered astrology as defined by Dr. Marc Edmund Jones is an optional pursuit in this special studies group. Please contact the author if you are interested in this esoteric way. Further information is available at http://www.sabian.org/

SABIAN SYMBOLS IN CARD READING

We all live with symbols. Without exception, consciously or not, we all interpret symbols. We categorize those we meet with memories of others we have known and thus they take on the symbolism of those others, rightly or wrongly. Isn't it true that if someone reminds you of an old friend you find yourself more kindly disposed toward them, or if their name is the same as a former lover who hurt you, aren't you wary? When you see a rainbow aren't you uplifted? Maybe you even think of the covenant, and if your past holds experience with symbolism training maybe you think of the iris as well. (That beautiful flower is a symbol standing for the rainbow and that same covenant. Check your dictionary.)

So, knowing we already have some understanding and experience with symbols the next step is to take conscious control of this tool for interpreting life. The willy-nilly method described above isn't necessarily too accurate. It is for some and not for others. We need a more perfected method for using symbols consciously, constructively and accurately. Down through history we have, as human beings, been using various methods for doing this. History tells us that the ancients even read the entrails of slaughtered animals. (You will be happy to know I won't be recommending that particular method!) We read tea leaves and we have found meaning and significance in reading the bumps on a person's head! There is a wide history of various ways and means for making symbols talk to us and reveal greater implication than is perceived on the surface of things. Though we laugh at some of the methods used never the less there is relevance here. After all the famed Dr. Carl Jung devoted most of his last year of life to a book called *Man and his Symbols.* The history of the use of the cards teaches us that we do definitely have to have three things in order to develop and use this skill effectively. 1) We do need something to read. Entrails aside, we do have to have something to use as a medium or agency. Then 2) a structure is required, a pattern which will allow us to read the "whatever," and, finally, 3) we need a means of interpreting what is defined there. So, let us look first into what to read.

One of the more convenient and most facile ways to work with symbols is to use a deck of cards. This medium is already familiar to all of us as a means for playing various "games." Because of the convenience of the popular deck of cards, it has been used as a divinatory tool by the gypsies and many others. There is, too, the old Tarot deck with its pictures and medieval history but that isn't what we are talking about here although it has a valuable place. We are involved with the very simple and totally convenient fifty-two card deck familiar to every one of us. In a modern society where even our most advanced psychology has accepted divination as a means of getting in touch with our higher selves, there is no reason for anyone to deprive himself of the convenient assistance of a deeper and broader perspective on life and its problems. This is readily available in the symbolism that this ordinary deck of cards can make available to each one of us.

There is an established tradition of using cards for this purpose and there are the ways and means of doing this as well. This is the structure or pattern as mentioned under number 2. This allows for the "whatever" to be read. The structure or the ways and means of reading cards is a "layout" or "arcanum." This is nothing more than a prescribed procedure for laying down the cards. You could think of it as a house plan. The living room is here, the bedroom there, etc. In the layout, the card that is found in the living room will tell you all about the living room and the one in the bedroom gives information about that part of the house and so on. So the layout will be a means of allowing the cards to tell you about factors that matter to you. In the layout we will recommend in this book you will find just about every facet of your life identified within a 15-card design.

The third and last factor that is absolutely necessary to the use of this tool, is the meanings of the cards. Reading cards is exactly that, a tool for understanding life and yourself and the situations that you meet as you move through the adventure that living is meant to be. You have your cards and you have a design to lay them out in, but then what? What are they saying to you? The bulk of this book will be about that very thing. I will spend time on what each card is saying to you, explaining in narrative form exactly what each card is communicating about the "room" in which it is found. This book is arranged in such a fashion that you can use it as a reference resource when you are working with the cards. This way, there is no pressure on you to memorize these meanings because the convenient reference format makes it comfortable for you to learn them by using them and to learn them at your own pace. This will enable you to have full use of the interpretations from the beginning of your layout of the cards. In other words, you can start reading the cards immediately with your first use of the cards!

There is no way to learn how to use this tool other than to just do it. The format of this volume will allow you to enjoy this process from the very beginning. After all, it should be a pleasant experience. This is an aid not unlike going to an old and wise friend for counsel, and it is a rewarding experience as well as a most insightful one. Each time we move to the cards for insight and guidance, we come closer to a larger inclusion that is available to us. We break down the barriers of our own limitations and break free into a new realm of knowing and awareness. The more you use the cards, the more adept you will become. I recommend doing a layout everyday. You can do this in the morning asking what the day holds for you since each day holds a gift if we can but discern what it is. Likewise, you can review your day with the cards, asking for insight into the most significant factors in your experience during the day that is drawing to a close. We race through life and we tend to miss so much meaning and significance that is there for us, but if we play this game of life we can seek more from each day and find it! This is our life, yours and mine, and it is our privilege to make the most of it. We can make it a grand adventure, a magnificent journey if we choose to do so, but to do this we must maximize our experiences. We must allow those experiences to expand our awareness. To do a layout each day, either morning or evening, doesn't preclude your using the cards to clarify issues that emerge during a day or to seek guidance as to how to handle certain situations. Making the cards a convenient and wonderful assistance is what it is all about but, *never* put the power in the cards. The power is in you and your use of the meanings and your skill in interpreting the medium. You are far more than you know. The use of the cards will help you recognize this. You are not asking to be told what to do, you are asking for guidance and insight. The decisions are always yours.

The bulk of this book will be about the individual

cards as little messages to trigger a higher knowing within you. Each card description will include a scenario which is a trigger to your own intuition. These word pictures were originally given to us by Dr. Marc Edmund Jones and his work with a gifted psychic, Zoe Wells, in 1922. Dr. Jones was in need of a deeper insight into the fifty-two playing cards for the system of tarot that he was developing for himself, a system based on the work that a man named Sampson had done originally. In this cooperative effort Zoe Wells was enabled to bring us these symbolic pictures as Dr. Jones held up each card. These have now, in this book, been expanded to a simple little action scene. Each of these pages on the individual cards which follow holds the original work of Zoe Wells with its keyword immediately after the designation Symbolic which is directly under each card. Following that you will find the expanded version now being made public, which has proven to be of further usefulness as you are working with the cards.

Dr. Jones established a system of seven keywords for each of the cards, and these pages will include each of those seven levels and the accompanying keyword for each card. It will be up to you to determine which of these levels you will be working with when you ask your question. It is necessary that you exercise your free will and determine which of these approaches will be your focus. This is a requisite, because the keywords on each level are related to the little scenario that is the key. There is a different use of the concept on each of the designated levels, and the advisement obtained will differ, depending upon which of these seven approaches is chosen. You will have at the top the Symbolic level and its picture and scenario as well as a keyword. It is recommended that initially you practice with this level for a little bit, at least, to become familiar with the "feel" of the card meanings. Thereafter, you are free to choose from the levels termed Superficial, Symbolic, Signature, Abstract, Ritualistic, Astrological or Brotherhood, depending on which you feel to be relevant to the question you are holding in consciousness. There will be those among you who will immediately perceive a correlation here with the chakric centers, and, if it is helpful for you to incorporate this knowledge in this practice, then that is encouraged. As well, there may be those of you who are familiar with the Theosophical system of levels and planes, and again if this has meaning for you then by all means include its use. In essence, whatever has meaning to you can become a part of this system of attribution to the cards.

First, you will wish to choose a card to represent yourself, and in time there may be other individuals represented among the cards, usually through the face cards. This more personalized use of the card can only expand its effectiveness through use. The cards become your own as you perceive in the stories and the keywords your own personal experience and your particular relevance and significance. These factors become the means by which the game of life truly becomes an art of living in your hands. Absolutely any card may be chosen to represent you — as long as it speaks to you in some way. Maybe you just like it or the little scenario involved appeals to you. If nothing of this nature emerges, you can take a traditional approach and look to the queens if you are a woman or girl or to the kings if you are a man and the jacks if you are a younger man. The historical use of the cards suggests you never change this once it is chosen, but this is your "game" and you get to play it your way. Always remember that.

Now, of course, there was a method in my madness when I suggested you find a card to represent yourself. To do this, it would seem that you might well have strolled through the pages pertaining to the cards themselves and thus you would have been exposed to the seven levels and the little scenarios and developed or recognized some "feeling" for what they are all about. This is good for it is the familiarizing of yourself with the ideas involved with each one of the cards that makes them "work" effectively. This is the reason for the advisement to use the cards regularly for the skill builds and becomes more powerful with each reading and use. You can see with this that the cards become a very personal experience and a medium that assists you in living the adventure of your life. Thus, it is advised that you never allow another to interpret a layout that you have brought to focus with a question and laid out. The cards are going to reflect your mind set through your subjective experience of them, and no other can know what that is. They will have their experience with the cards as well as with life but that is for them to use for themselves as yours is for you. We are individuals, and we grow and develop in our own uniqueness and we must respect one another and give full regard to each of us.

USING CARDS FOR DIVINATION

The ordinary deck of playing cards most commonly used for playing Bridge or Poker has the added advantage of being readily at hand in most every home or local drug store. So, for our purposes we will use a deck of ordinary playing cards. There is no need for expensive decks unless you appreciate the art work and quality. There does have to be adequate slipperiness (to coin a term) in the deck to allow it to pass easily and swiftly one card over the other as you shuffle them in this manner. You pass the deck over and over itself and allow the cards to interpenetrate the deck as they will. You do not split the deck and bend the cards into one another by fanning the deck as is customary when playing games such as bridge or poker. So, find a deck you like that has a slippery surface and use it for divination until it becomes conditioned in ways that impede its purely chance performance. This means changing your deck fairly frequently when the cards become bent or sticky or in any way worn, and they no longer have the full fluidity that is the key to the operation of the chance element which is so important in this process. We must have full accessibility to total synchronicity. So change your deck as needed, remembering the power is not in the deck anyway. Using a new, fresh deck is never a problem other than insuring that it is adequately shuffled to totally remove the packaged sequential ordering.

If you have no experience with this way of shuffling a deck it might be well to practice this a bit just to insure you are comfortable with the process. Hold the deck in your left hand with a long edge up. With your right hand, take hold of the deck as if to lift it up with your thumb at one end and two or three fingers at the other. Gently lift with your fingers, not gripping too hard. This allows some cards to be lifted and others to remain. Put those that lift to the front of the deck. Repeat this process until the deck is "set." Some recognize this "set" in the cards when the deck suddenly feels heavy. Others know it to be "done," so to speak, when the cards seem to "stick" as you go to lift them and none come. Whatever you discover as the means of recognizing that the shuffling is finished is fine, but do develop your sensitivity and find the method of "knowing" that works for you. Experiment and practice and you will recognize what is your signature or indication of "ready." As you do this, remember that because this is an art and not a science, any "accidents" have dramatic meanings. This means that when you drop a card, it isn't just ineptitude or carelessness. It is signature, a sign. This gives relevance to cards that fall out from the deck or that act in any way differently from the norm. From the first moments of your work with the cards, you wish to develop a very communicative relationship with them. They will speak to you in many ways. It is up to you to observe, to watch, to perceive, not just hurry on through as if to get something done or finished. A very relaxed and "easy does it" mode of operation is what is most successful here. A phrase Dr. Jones used in another context is valuable to me here and that is to work with an "unhurried eagerness of spirit."

THE LAYOUT OR ARCANUM

Having practiced a bit with the cards to insure that you are comfortable with the shuffling process, we can now talk about the actual Arcanum. This begins with your question in mind and the level of meaning chosen and set in your mind as you start your shuffle. As you approach this key stage of this process dignity is needed. There needs to be a sense of the touch with a higher level of consciousness, and this is facilitated when you come to the process with respect. Some find it helpful to pause here and silently call on those invisible sponsors that assist or to speak a silent word of prayer. It is helpful to sit up straight and maintain a posture of poised anticipation with your feet flat on the floor to ensure a touch with a basic foundation. This position is a metaphor for maintaining the posture of being in touch with the earth even when you are on the third floor of a building.

In this position pick up the cards and shuffle, but, *most important,* do this with your question in mind. Think this out very carefully as the success of your work is totally dependent on the clarity of your inquiry and your ability to maintain your focus on this question and not lose it as you read your layout! Prediction is possible with cards but not necessarily reliable, and it isn't really desirable. To know what will happen can be helpful, but it puts you in the role of the victim more often than not. What is more wonderful is to find assistance and insight and even higher guidance in how to deal with your life. So my recommendation is to keep the action in your hands and make your inquiries more along the lines of, "What would be the result of taking a certain action?" If you have no action in mind or perhaps the issue isn't one where you have that option, then you might wish to try something like: "Can you help me understand what is needed here or can you give me guidance for handling this issue?"

Now, it is absolute fact that the stronger the need, the more powerful the layout, but you can't deal only with crisis! There are disciplines that can be incorporated into your life that can be infinitely rewarding, and if you are sincere and genuinely seeking to improve your awareness and productivity and even your sense of your own spirituality and its role in your daily life, the power will be there and will be reflected in the cards. One of these exercises is to do a layout each day as mentioned earlier. If your schedule allows for this in the morning, then focus on advisement for how to discover the best of this day or the gift that it holds for you. Now remember, this is a very difficult assignment since you have no real focus other than just the day — the whole span of twenty-four hours, but if through the day you listen and watch and check and review, this exercise will build your skill more rapidly and effectively than any other technique. The retrospective approach, done at the end of the day in review but using the same question, is equally effective and in some ways easier because you have the awareness of the events of the day. This isn't always helpful because having already had the experience you come to the arcanum with preconceived views, and if the gift revealed is one you haven't seen, you may be standing in your own way. This then becomes a difficult exercise in clearing your discernment — but an infinitely valuable one.

There should be no lack of questions for the student of reading cards because every life, whether at home and with children, or in the marketplace and the public, or in the office and the business of the day or whatever, can be handled with greater awareness and found to be more meaningful to the individual. This is your objective, in an overall sense, when you start to play this game of life. Don't hesitate to check out your conditioned point of view in issues of your everyday life. You may find you can include a whole lot more insight in living your everyday life than you have had up to this point. There is enlarged perspective to be gained if you just open yourselves up to it. This is a time in the history of humankind that can certainly use an expanded consciousness — in fact, it may be imperative for us to gain it! Naturally, the real problems, the crisis points, the challenges of our lives offer us the greatest of all opportunities to bring through to our lives an improved and more perceptive way of going by using the card's messages and expanded insights.

Next, it is necessary to choose which level of interpretation you feel is appropriate to your particular question. A study of these levels is a start to your personal intuition. As mentioned earlier, do be willing to use any experience and knowledge of your own and to find its value as applied in these choices.

THE SEVEN LEVELS OF INTERPRETATION

Starting with Symbolic allows you to develop familiarity with the basic scenarios, but the decision as to which level to use is yours. There are clues to how the various levels might be found useful, though, and we will discuss those to start off.

SUPERFICIAL is the name that Dr. Jones gave the first level, and I respect that and retain it, however in my mind it has become more like Fundamental. This level to me is very basic, and I use this when I am in need of purely pragmatic guidance as to how to deal with the nitty-gritty of life. This is the purely practical insight on living with life as it really is and the problems of utilitarian application that constantly emerge in daily situations. Much of the guidance deals with relationships and most of life is that. We deal with other people and we deal with issues, and, either way the dealing is primarily a matter of how we relate.

SYMBOLIC we have already discussed to some extent but in addition we can view it as the most universal of the levels. Here is where we have the greatest contact with a breadth of view or a more generalized perspective. This generalized broad view gives this level the broadest application of all the levels. In particular, it seems appropriate to the more personal facets of our lives, the issues to do with security such as home, surroundings and well-being, and our outreach from that point within ourselves.

SIGNATURE is a very psychic level because here we deal with the meaning of the outer events rather than the events themselves. This can be the sudden, unexpected impact of what can be a trivial event in practical fact but one which we know is highly significant in meaning. Yet we need help in interpreting that meaning to ourselves.

ABSTRACT is the level I use very much as is indicated in the title. I go here when I need to understand. This provides a purely intellectual understanding of any issue or situation. When I am at a loss to figure out what is involved, or really at stake, so to speak, clarification comes in on this level.

RITUALISTIC touches back to the old, old traditions of the Tarot and catches for us, in this updated version, the deeply rooted archetypes that have been established in the subconscious. This level can evoke these for our use now. You might find this level of value when there are issues of control or authority involved.

ASTROLOGICAL takes you into trends with a vision of the future and the possibilities involved in that longer range view of life. This level can be most meaningful in that context. When using this level keep in mind the life cycles and the rites of passage and the milestones.

BROTHERHOOD is the most exalted of the levels, and it is dynamically involved when you are asking advisement or guidance from pure spirit, your spiritual guides or however you think of your access to a higher consciousness. This is particularly relevant when you are involved with your life's mission and those areas of your true dedication and commitment in life.

You will notice as you use the sheets that follow, one for each of the fifty-two cards, that each level is related to the others, yet has a perspective of its own. This is the reason for setting the level from which you intend to read your layout, prior to even shuffling the cards. Once your question is phrased and hopefully written down with a date and time entered (for future reference), you should have your chosen level in mind as you go to shuffling the cards.

As you have noticed, the slight variance in the frame of reference in the different levels can allow a card to be a very positive indicator on one level and a cautionary or go-easy indicator on another level, all within the same card and the same scenario. This is no doubt one of the beauties of this system devised by Dr. Jones because it gives such an individual approach for each one operating the system and dealing with the cards. Your perspective is so wonderfully served when you choose your level of meaning ahead of shuffling.

LAYING OUT THE ARCANUM

Having studied the levels and made your choice and holding your comfortable but erect posture as you hold your question strongly in mind, you pick up the cards. Shuffle, paying close attention to any "accident" of fall out card or things such a card seeming to "feel" sticky or maybe one just "hanging around." All of these and many other experiences can have meaning for you as you progress through to the ideal shuffle and your arcanum. When the deck feels heavy or you spot a key indicator of "readiness," whatever you find this to be as you practice with the cards, or any other psychic indicators that you develop, then you cut the cards with the query, "Is the deck ready?" Now, many operators merely go by the simple device of when cutting a red card it means yes and a black no. If black then continue shuffling and cutting until the cut is red. Having the deck ready, you now can lay down the arcanum. (Remember everything to do with using the cards involves your sensitivity, so you may develop cards of special meaning to you that are exceptions to this rule of red indicating that the cards are ready.)

When you have reached this point, it is wonderfully important to have paper and pen ready because you will find that if you fail to record a layout you will come to regret it! It just seems to be an esoteric fact that the one you don't write down is the one that you will need to refer to for some reason later. Actually, it is often necessary to go back and renew and review the insights gained! Make a record of it and date it, noting the question and the time very carefully! (There is a worksheet included at the back of this volume for this purpose.) Your first step now is to make a notation as to the cut card.

Take the deck in your left hand with the spots (number) side down and put down one third of the deck. Move your hand to the right, and put down another third. Finally, again to the right, then lay down the balance of the cards.

This apportionment of the cards into thirds is, of course, approximate and will vary with the time and question but your objective is to keep the cards in the one-third mode. If that slips, then it has meaning. However, if you are just careless or thoughtless, it doesn't. It is at this point that the discipline of working with the cards enters the picture. A controlled and disciplined methodology is vital for the chance factors to operate fully. If carelessness is the mode, then the occasional slippage will lack meaning as it is the consistent norm. So keep a structure and establish a ritual with your work with the cards. Don't make this a tedious or burdensome task, but do let it be one to which you bring your full attention and total concentration. This is merely the respect you must have for your own higher capacities.

Now pick up the first pile of cards. This pile contains the information about the past that is relevant to your question. Dealing from the top, lay out four cards from left to right and replace the pack face up. Now pick up the second pile of cards. This pile contains the information about the present that is relevant to your question. Dealing from the top, lay out four cards immediately underneath the first four. Now pick up the last pile and deal four cards immediately under the first two rows. This is the future of your question. See Figure 1.

Figure 1

Laying Out The Arcanum

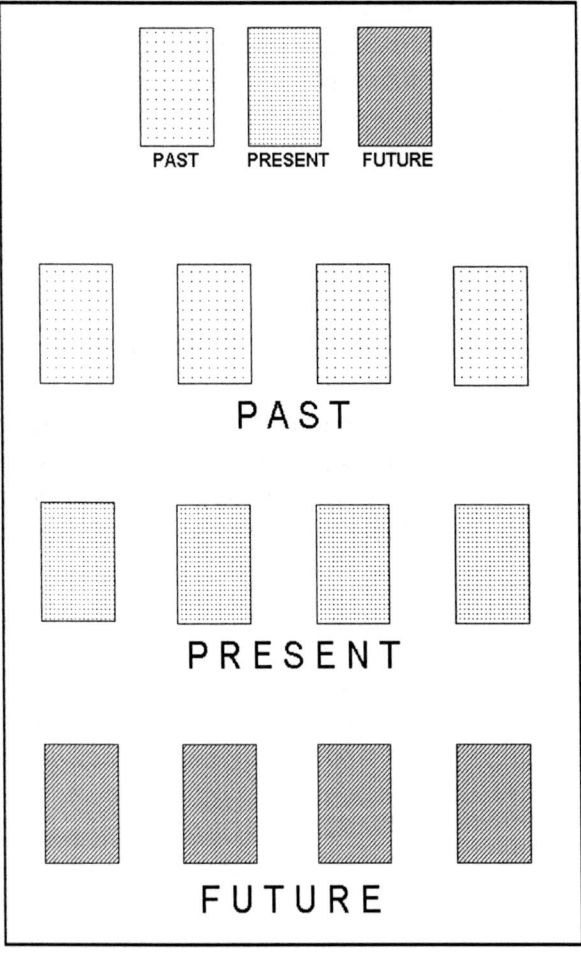

Now you have three piles of cards each face up across the upper register of your arcanum, and these represent, moving from left to right, the past, the present and the future. This upper register is the whole story of the past, present and future in capsule form, a full overview. There is much more detail to gained from the cards directly underneath as you have four cards that further explain the past. Underneath that you have four cards which further explain the present of your question, and immediately below those you have four more cards which further explain the future of your question. Please see Figures #1 and #2.

Figure 2

How to Read the Arcanum

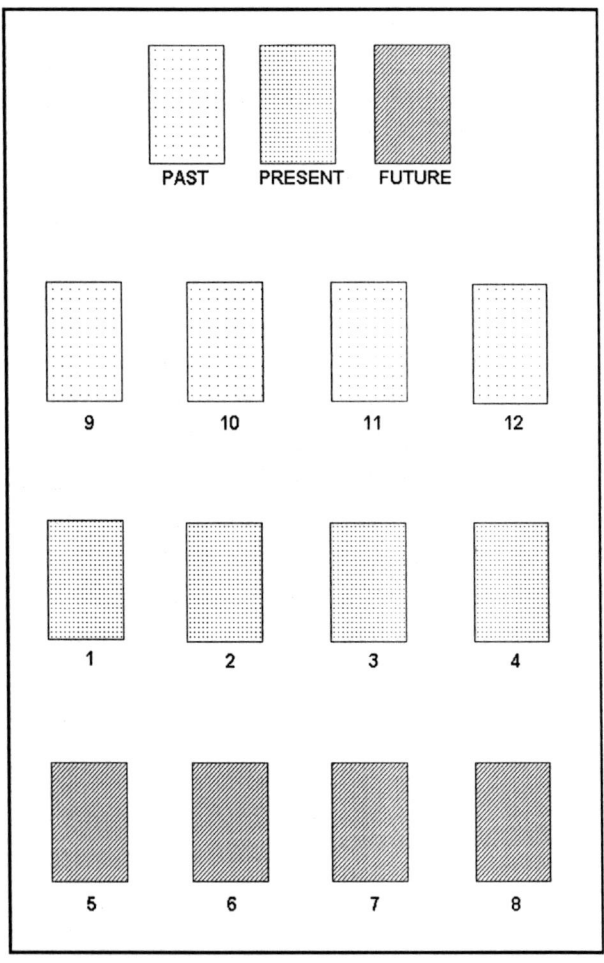

As you study Figure #2, you discover that each of the rooms in the house is numbered and these numbers correspond to the meanings described in HOW TO READ THE ARCANUM on page thirty. The first block on HOW TO READ THE ARCANUM tells you about the cut card and then we speak of The Keynote card but please let us go into that a little bit later. We will do it shortly. Right now the idea is to become familiar with the twelve rooms in the house. The four that have to do with the past, 9, 10, 11 and 12. The four that have to do with the present 1, 2, 3 and 4 and lastly the four that have to do with the future 5, 6, 7 and 8. Those of you who have astrological training have no doubt recognized the twelve houses of the astrological horoscope and this is good, as you will be able to incorporate your astrological knowledge into your use of the cards. Use a little care, though, and become familiar with these notes, because the actual meanings are a little different in perspective. From this point on, we will refer to the rooms in the house by the numbers of each one; for example the 9th will be referred to as the Motivation that led you to ask the question. Just how effective or negative this motivation may be is what the 9th house card will tell you. You can discover if your mind set needs to be changed or if your thinking is fine as to what led you to seek advisement concerning this matter. Then you move to the 10th. This will give you a picture of exactly what is controlling the entire issue and if it is in a mode that will allow you to work with this issue effectively, or if it needs to be altered in some way. Then comes the look to the future wish that you are holding, the objective you seek in the 11th. Next comes the 12th and here you can clarify exactly what it is you can accomplish with this issue. Maybe it holds even more than you had thought or perhaps it is blocked in ways that you cannot overcome. All of this is read in the light of what the upper register (top three cards) past card is telling you. In each instance, that upper register gives you the overview, whether of past, present or future.

You then move to the present card and the four cards of 1st, 2nd, 3rd and 4th positions as the means of working with it right now. The 1st one gives you the most important key of all, because the 1st card is the focus of the matter and indicates how it can be approached. The 2nd will tell you about what you have to use or work with in connection with this. The 3rd is most interesting because here you discover what, if anything, is going on or is involved that you may not be seeing or considering. The 4th is the actual strength of the matter, and, in many ways, this is the card that tells you just how much can be accomplished with this issue at this time.

Then move to the future. Read the upper register card and then work through the 5th, 6th, 7th and 8th cards as they describe that future card. The 5th is how you move ahead, your next move. The 6th is the actual effort, the hard work you must put forth to accomplish anything. The 7th is how you gain cooperation, and the 8th is how you fit this issue into the larger pattern of your life and the lives of the others involved.

Please study this review with Figure 2 and the **HOW TO READ THE ARCANUM** sheet which follows.

HOW TO READ THE ARCANUM
(Use with Figure 2)
The rooms of the house

The Cut Card indicates the state of mind in respect to this issue. How positive you are about it or how you see it.

The Keynote Card indicates a key to dealing with this issue and is read combined with the Cut Card.

The Past: This describes the past in respect to this issue in general, overall terms.

The Present: This describes the present in respect to this issue in general, overall terms.

The Future: This describes the future in respect to this issue in general, overall terms.

9 - The Concept: This describes the state of your understanding in respect to the question. Are you really in full possession of what is involved or do you need to further investigate or shift your perspective?

10 - The Authority: What is in control here? How much authority do you have or just what is controlling the situation as it has been set up to this point?

11 - The Visualization: What is being hoped for or what you are reaching for or striving to achieve as things stand to this point.

Sabian Symbols in Card Reading 31

12 - The Support: What is supporting you or sustaining you as you have set things up so far in respect to this issue.

1 - The Focus of the matter, the real issue as it stands now in respect to your question.

2 - The Fluidity of resources you have to work with in connection with the question.

3 - The Sensitiveness involved: Here you find what you may be missing or overlooking in regard to your question. What you need to pay more attention to in respect to the whole thing.

4 - The Strength of the matter: Just what are you standing on as a power or a weakness.

5 - The Control involved: Here is described your first step into the future of this issue. What it is you need to be expressing.

6 - The Application: This describes the actual work or effort that you need to do or take in respect to this issue.

7 - The Cooperation: Here is shown the cooperation you can capitalize upon to expedite your issue, or the lack of cooperation.

8 - The Realignment: This describes the resources of that cooperation and what may be available in this new mode. In addition here is shown how well it fits into the larger pattern.

THE SUITS

Down through history the meaning of the suits has been derived from their correspondence to the four elements. Clubs are the fire representatives, diamonds are the earth, spades are air and hearts are water. Those of you who are familiar with astrological meanings will find in this a familiar note, and those of you who are not will easily see the relevance as introduced here. The suits give you a clue as to how to handle the situation that you are asking about via the position in the various rooms of the arcanum with each individual card. As well, you will find that as you are developing your Individual Keynote for the arcanum {described just further on}, you will count the cards to find the preponderance of a particular suit. This gives you an immediate insight into the totality of the layout and the question being addressed. The first house of the arcanum is describing the focus of the issue at hand so the suit that is represented there is an important clue as to how to deal with the question at hand. When you find that Clubs are in a focal position (either by being in the majority or relevant to a particular house or especially when in the first position), then advisement is to handle this situation with full vitality and effort focused in activity. A very direct involvement with what is taking place around you is necessary. This is a time when you are able to call life into the fullness of its potentials. When it is Diamonds that are focal in any of these ways, then it is the practical approach to the issue that matters and must be maintained. This indicates that you must be dealing with down-to-earth issues of life and that attention to these is a positive at this time in respect to your inquiry. When Spades are the dynamic, then it is the thought processes that are the most relevant. Your intellectual evaluations and your ability to formulate ideas and to use concepts becomes highly significant. This is a matter of your willingness to remain fluid and see various points of view and, most important, to allow new insights to enter your consciousness and to expand your understanding. When Hearts are the key, then it is a time to work from a sense of unity and inner completeness in which your creative awareness is heightened and you are able to find and use all that is available to you in consciousness.

INTERPRETATION OF THE CARDS

Now that you have a grasp of what the rooms of the house really seek to tell you through the arcanum and have a feeling for the suits, you are now ready to discover the real substance of this game of life -- the meanings of the individual cards themselves. This is truly an everlasting study as there isn't anything in life that cannot be added to the card meanings. This will become a personal experience for you as you work with the cards themselves and as the various subtleties of your own consciousness start to speak to you through the medium of the cards. However, it is necessary to have a basis for this journey that you will be making for the rest of your life! This basis is contained in the pages that follow that are really the major contribution of this little book.

Each card has a scenario to be read and this evokes a response from within you. Thus you have a sense of what the card is truly speaking to you about. Then there are seven levels of meaning. As has been mentioned earlier, it is your job to choose which of these levels you will be working with before you lay down the cards.

It has been suggested that you start with Symbolic which is the level of meaning that is addressed via the little scenarios because this gives you a touch with the key to the card itself. This is the level of insight that allows your empathetic response the greatest degree of play. If you familiarize yourself with this initially, it will stand you in good stead as a base for the rest of the insights of the other levels.

Now we are ready to do a layout, and, of course we instantly find we haven't covered the Individual Keynote, so here it is:

INDIVIDUAL KEYNOTE

To find the Keynote card just count the number of red cards and the number of black in your layout. Take the one that is the greater and count the number of clubs and spades if black, hearts and diamonds if red. Say you have 10 red and, since that's more than the 5 black, red is your suit. Then you count and you have 6 hearts and four diamonds so 6 hearts are the greater -- thus the six of hearts is your keynote card. This is read combined with the cut card as an overview of your whole layout. This will be illustrated in the example layout coming up.

As you embark on this journey, it is a very good thing to make a record of your experience. This means writing down your arcana. I know, I know, it is a major pain but you will really be glad you did. In an attempt to facilitate your doing this, I am including here a worksheet which has helped me along the way. You may in time, revert to a shorthand of your own and that's grand, or as some students prefer, you may stay with this format if it pleases you exactly as it is. That is equally grand. So here is the worksheet, and into the bargain let's include a sample layout so you can kind of feel into just what is being done here. Now, instantly with that statement, there is the need to add that this will be one person's way with the cards, and it is a wonderfully magical way FOR ME. Thus it can be shared with you as an example, but it must not be considered the ONLY WAY! You must develop your own wonderfully magical way. It may be similar to mine or it may be very different. It is in the finding of it and developing of it that you will make this game your own and touch the joy of it all. So, in the spirit of sharing, here is the worksheet with an example layout. At the end of the book you will find a blank worksheet that you may copy for your own use.

EXAMPLE LAYOUT

Of course, now we need a question. I've been waiting for this experiment and hope to have fun along with you in asking higher levels of consciousness to aid in this process and give us insight into exactly how this system of divination can be made a real adventure and a skill in your expansion of consciousness. How best can you be aided at this time of starting to work with this book and this system? Okay, that's good. We have a question and we can focus on that, but along with the question we need to confirm and affirm which level of the seven meanings will be used for the interpretation of this arcanum. Because we are really seeking higher guidance for all concerned here, it is without doubt the Brotherhood level that will be most appropriate. Now, if one of you is vitally interested in another of the levels in respect to this question, then it is a fine exercise to go ahead and work out the interpretation on that level for your instruction and information. For the purposes of illustration, I will go to my quiet place and concentrate and shuffle and bring back to this book the layout, and we can try the worksheet for this first time as a means of both interpretation and as a means of record keeping.

Sabian Symbols in Card Reading

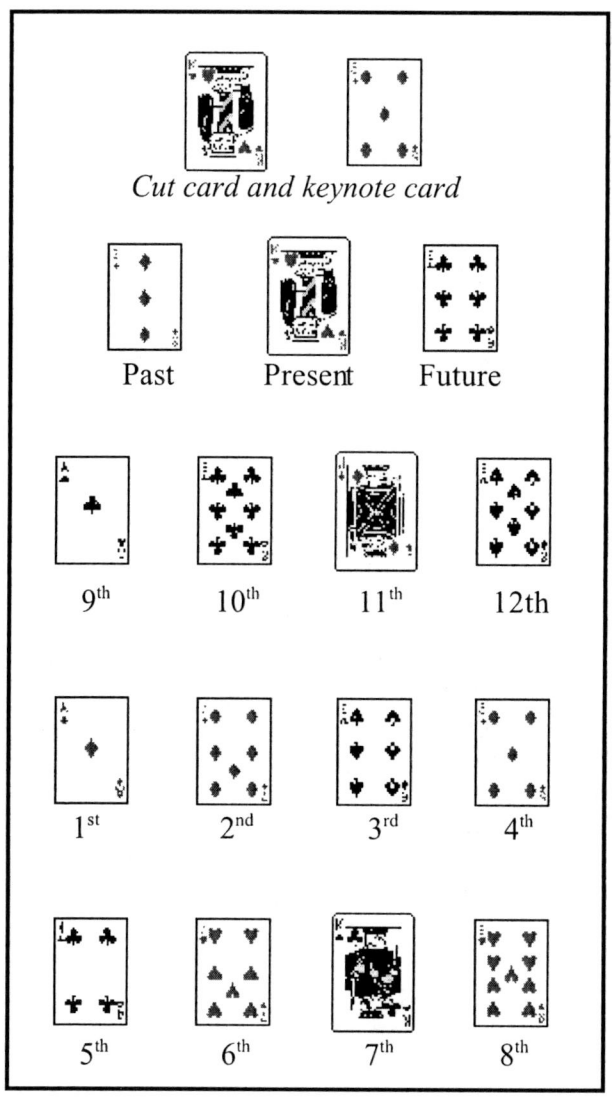

DATE: 3/14/97 TIME: 3:42 p.m.

QUESTION: *How best can you be aided at this time of starting to work with this book and this system?* LEVEL: 7

THE CUT CARD IS AND SAYS TO
REMEMBER: *K♡* <u>Retrospection</u>*: Go back over your layouts*
 RED: *8* BLACK: 7 KEYNOTE: 5♦
<u>Agency</u> *as that is the <u>agency</u>. The means of your learning.*

THE PAST IS *3♦ <u>Reciprocity</u>* A MATTER OF: *your working with the book in cooperation. Your work + its information.*

09 - *A* ♣ THE UNDERSTANDING IS INVOLVED WITH: *Where you <u>place</u> your layout - which level.*

10 - *8* ♣ THAT WHICH IS IN CONTROL IS: *Your <u>mission</u> in life. The really important contribution that you can make.*

11 - *J* ♦ REACH FOR: *The <u>designation</u>, your being named to the job, the work, the effort and the skill.*

12 - 8♠ THE SUPPORT IS IN THE: *Orders you receive, the instruction.*

SUMMARY: *Be willing to work with the system. Your real work in life can be facilitated if you are willing to accept the importance of your own role in life. There is special instruction for you here.*

THE PRESENT IS: K♥ *This echoes the cut and reminds you to review your work and your experience.*

01 - A♦ FOCUS ON: *The new start and your assertiveness as you move into this new effort.*

02 - 7♦ VIA: *Using the cards as a recourse, turn to them for guidance as often as is needed and wanted.*

03 - 6♠ DON'T OVERLOOK AND STAY SENSITIVE TO: *An overshadowing, a strong psychic influence.*

04 - 5♦ YOUR STRENGTH IS IN THE: *Agency, the means of doing all this which is the cards and the book.*

SUMMARY: *Make a strong start and let the cards become a real recourse for you. With this there can be a really psychic development emerging but you must use the means for developing it which is your work with the book and the cards.*

THE FUTURE IS: *6 ♣ The process of moving from knowing to becoming - it's time to walk your talk!*

05 - *4 ♣* START WITH: *Paying attention to your impressions and release all fear.*

06 - *7♥* MAKE AN EFFORT TO: *Develop this system as a real resource for yourself and maybe even make touch with me as this is my card.*

07 - *K♣* THE GREATER OPPORTUNITY IS IN: *The authorship, so the book matters but so do you as the author of your own destiny.*

08 - *9♥* VIA: *Your recommittal, your willingness to commit yourself again and again to this effort.*
SUMMARY: *Start out knowing you have the ability and you can do it and then keep up the effort. Contact the book as often as needed and maybe even the author and know that this effort will help you take control of your life.*

CONCLUSIONS ARE: There may be more here for you than you have even suspected. Give it a good chance!

The Four Worlds confirm and add:

The World of Self	The World of Responsibility	The World of Relationship	The World of Spirit
09 Fire	10 Fire	11 Earth	12 Air
01 Earth	02 Earth	03 Air	04 Earth
05 Fire	06 Water	07 Water	08 Water
Use spirit with practical it	*Use spirit and make practical use of the feelings*	*Use practicality with thought & feeling*	*Use ideas with practicality & feeling*

THE FOUR WORLDS

I know, you got to the end of the example layout on the worksheet and discovered something titled the **FOUR WORLDS**, saying this confirms and adds yet no one had mentioned this! What is it? Well, it's an additional technique that you can use if you care to. Its purpose is to give you an additional check on what you have concluded from the original layout. As well, it can expand that insight with additional factors. See Figure 3 for an illustration of the FOUR WORLDS.

The Four Worlds are a part of Marc Edmund Jones' astrological techniques[1] and they can be applied in this Tarot context wonderfully well. The illustration on the example question merely uses the keywords for the suits involved and while this very simple approach can be helpful, it can be expanded as much as you might care to take the time to do.

The World of Self tells you about yourself or about the person who is asking the question. It will speak of how you are in this situation. First, it gives you the past that you are leaning on -- this is shown by the 9th house of your understanding. If it is a red card then you may feel you are in pretty good rapport with the reality of the issue. If it is black, then you need to reconsider your attitude and approach. In the 1st you

---

[1] *Astrology, How and Why it Works*

Figure 3

The Four Worlds

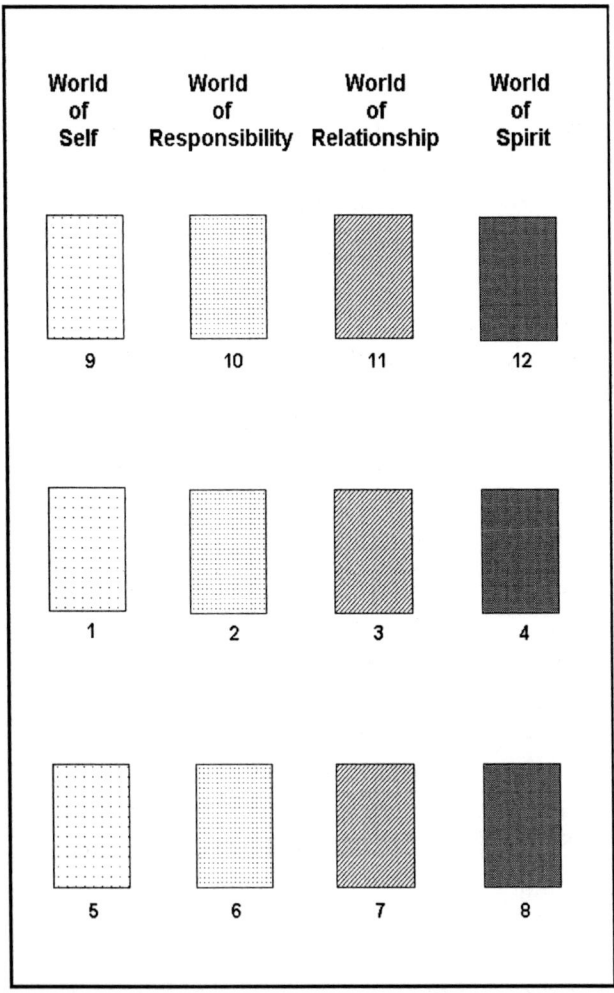

see yourself and the question and it too tells you a great deal about your mode of operation in getting whatever is concerned here off the ground. Study this placement assiduously both here and in the arcanum itself. Here it can describe you very accurately or the person asking the question. See if you are described as you would wish to be. Again, if it is a red card, then you may well be in very good order aligned correctly for the demands or opportunities of the situation asked about. However, if it is a black card, then consider a possible adjustment in your approach. Now, immediately here you see why it is so very important to have your question clearly in mind and hopefully have it written down. If your question involves shifting your position or attitude or ways and means, then the black focus is most appropriate. If the question is involved with maintaining the status quo or the familiar situation, then black cards here will suggest you may have to make an adjustment or shift your attention in some manner in order to deal with this particular situation really well. In the example, we find that the 9th is one of adjustment, and so it reveals to you the need to include new ideas and some difference in your thinking. This isn't surprising as this whole question involves a new technique. The 1st house is indicating you are in a fortunate position to deal with this issue of learning, but it reminds you to stay practical with it all and not get too unrealistic about it. This is a very practical skill and you need to approach it as such. The 5th house indicates your self-expression— your ability to move out and away from the more conditioned ways of going that may have been taught to you along the way. It is the next step as you move into the future, and in the Four Worlds this shows you your first step in this regard. In the example layout you are shown to be in a change mode and using spirit, so this is wonderful. This is most certainly what is needed, to include all possible new ideas in your repertoire!

To summarize, **The World of Self** in the example arcanum indicates you are in a change mode but with the focus a practical factor that you have well in hand. All in all, a kind of ideal mode for a new adventure!

The World of Responsibility shows you all about your function in the world. Here are the houses that speak of your actual position and work situation in respect to the question. Starting with the 10th house, this indicates how much control you have over the situation that is being asked about. In the example layout this is indicated as your mission in life and is a black card; thus you can feel the shift going on as you move into a closer association with your real work in the world and this life. We next move to the 2nd house which speaks to you of the rewards that are there to be used. The 2nd house can be very informative in questions that require a strength of resource in any way, whether this be actual finances or allies. In the example, the card here is the 7 of Diamonds and shows you to be in command of a very real practical resource of genuine value. This is a superb indication. The 6th house will indicate what the actual effort is that you need to put forth here to accomplish the desired result. Always remember as you read these that the red cards indicate a more "in the flow" of the situation and the black show the need for a shifting energy to be accommodated. The example layout is most reassuring in its red card here.

To summarize, **The World of Responsibility** in the example arcanum indicates you have a change going on as far as what and how you wish to control your life but that you have everything you need to do it with and to perform as you wish.

The World of Relationship indicates everything to do with the cooperation or lack of it that is available to you from the other or others involved in the situation asked about. The 11th is the house of objectives and goals and as well indicates the friends that are or might be involved. The red cards show you to be supported by friends if you need to be and that your objectives are in order. If black here, then study it out to see what is involved. It can mean your objectives are changing and thus you may need a new group affiliation or some new associations to expedite the new goals. Next comes the 3rd house, and this is a matter of all the conveniences that may be at hand and of all communication issues as well as siblings but most important, is its indication of what you might be overlooking. This means that the card here shows you what to give further attention to, if it is black, and if red you are shown to be pretty well aware of what is involved, at least for the moment. In the example layout there is indication of much more psychic sensitivity and assistance through that mode of operation than you have known up to this time, so there is hidden talent lingering around with this question. Finally, in the World of Relationship is the 7th house and here is the cooperation directly with others and thus the greater opportunity that can be realized in respect to what is being asked about. In the example this is the relationship with this book itself, perhaps even the author.

To summarize, **The World of Relationship** in the example arcanum shows your expectation and aspiration to be all you expect things to be and then allows for change and development of new relationships to accomplish this. One possibility here is the book itself and those that have and are attached to working with this system of card reading. Then there is shown the very wonderful possibility of invisible presences of a beneficial nature becoming involved if you really wish to apply yourself to your real work in the world. The past of this layout which isn't involved in the Four Worlds is the card that I use to stand for the Sabian Assembly described in the

Prologue in this book. This is very logical because this system of card reading is a result of the work that was done by Dr. Jones who created the Sabian Assembly.

The World of Spirit shows the depth of you and your spiritual endeavor in respect to the question asked. It starts with the 12th house as indicating your invisible support and your hidden motivations in respect to the whole idea. In the example layout this is unusually strong in that it shows a whole new perspective possible for you as you accept arcane instruction. This world then moves to the 4th house which shows the real soul strength of this whole proposition and the in-depth security that you can draw from and use. In the example this is fortunate and described as an agency of some kind which is a matter of the means of doing something. The red card indicates that this is already there for you. Last, we come to the 8th house which indicates the future potential of the spiritual development possible here and this is a matter of your willingness to recommit yourself to the disciplines and instructions involved here. It hints that you may have been involved before with something of this nature and it is time now to recommit yourself to the path.

In the example arcanum **The World of Spirit** indicates a depth of potential for you to capitalize upon if you will accept the instruction and make the necessary use of the ways and means of doing it. This requires a real commitment.

I hope this helps you see how you can use this technique of **The Four Worlds** to check your arcanum and even gain new insight as you view the question from these new perspectives. It is your choice as to whether or not to use this technique. Sometimes you may wish to and sometimes not. It is a matter of how important is the question to you and how much time is available and even your own personal likes and dislikes. There are many techniques and methods that can be added to your repertoire and it is a matter of which factors speak to you and how you incorporate them into your system of using the cards.

Now, before I turn you over to the balance of this book which, as you know, is all about the individual cards, I have one, special, last card to talk about first.

THE JOKER

Every deck of cards has a Joker or maybe two and normally in our work with the symbolism of the cards we don't include the Joker. It is used as a cover for the deck so the top card isn't observable until the Joker is removed. Then, before the cards are lifted to be shuffled the Joker is removed and set aside.

As with all things, occasionally the order of doing is interrupted and the Joker ends up in the pack of cards and in your layout! When this happens, it has special meaning and needs special attention. The Joker stands for the unusual, the different and thus, when it appears in your layout, something is going on that holds a whole new potential of some nature. The mutation or 'sport' is a possibility here and that means a completely new and different eventuality. This is stronger than just black cards indicating a shift. This is a completely new birth of something that hasn't been seen before — so, if this happens, pay attention to your Joker and where it is and just what it is striving to communicate to you. It is telling you that there is a whole new possibility in your life potential!

Well, that's it, folks. From here it is entirely up to you! You can make this the most exciting game you have ever played as you make your life a greater success and your living more fulfilling. You can be in real touch with your higher self and the wisdom of the ages if you care to develop the use of the cards. I wish you well and remind you of the worksheet at the end of this book if you care to copy it — Oh, and take a look at the seal at the end of the Prologue that goes with the Jack of Spades. If any of you are familiar with it and can tell me more about it, please do.

Have a magnificent adventure from here on!

NOTES

NOTES

THE INDIVIDUAL CARD DESCRIPTIONS

Symbolic
Ace of Diamonds: *Plenty* "Unformed matter in great abundance."

He stared out at the white expanse of landscape the snow had created and the words of his teacher echoed in his ears. "Consciousness is reality." He saw how the unformed matter of the snow took on the form of whatever was its base. The analogy was quite good he thought; Reality acts as the snow does, it follows the outline that the individual consciousness holds as the mold. Our expectations are our mold. We can change our reality if we can change the meanings we assign to our experiences. It stands to reason that if we change our attitude about a situation, we will change the reality, just as the next snowfall will take the shape of any new fence or house build on the landscape. A new beginning is possible now.

Superficial: *Gift:* "Unto every one that hath {in consciousness} shall be given, and he shall have abundance; but from him that hath not {in consciousness} shall be taken away even that which he hath." Matthew 25.29 A new beginning is now possible.

Signature: *Beginning:* Defined as: "to start doing, acting, going, to get under way." Yes, you may now realign and start afresh. Move into the chosen reality through focusing your expectations as a mold for what you truly prefer rather than for what you fear.

Abstract: *Birth:* Defined as: "the beginning of anything." There can be a new beginning at any moment in any time -- if you alter your thinking, your state of mind, your expectation, you realign your world. For if you adjust the mold, the reality will follow.

Ritualistic: *Perception:* This becomes all important in the light of this understanding for it is as you perceive, or grasp mentally that you create. It is in your capacity to choose what is preferred and then train your perception to see as you choose to create, to follow that preference, that discernment. A new beginning can be seen.

Astrological: *Pleasure:* What is your pleasure? Your wish is a choice. Go for it! Be there. Choose happiness! Make a new start.

Brotherhood: *Assertion:* "The way to start is to start." Begin. It is in your hands and you have the ability to move ahead in the chosen manner. Go for it!

Symbolic

2 of Diamonds: *Spiritualization* "A right hand holding a scepter upside down."

She was young and lovely but more than that, she seemed a part of the scene. Her smile and high spirits matched the song of the birds and the lightness of her step mimicked the deer and the fawn. Her staff was merely a trimmed and smoothed sapling but it could have been made of gold and rubies as the sun hit its polished surface and set it to glowing. She pointed it to the skies in the joy of sheer livingness and pure *spirit* showered the world as she pointed it to earth.

Superficial: *Chance:* On a day like this anything can happen! Let the convergence emerge, the happening take place, the encounter become manifest! Here is the lucky meeting! Let serendipity work for you!

Signature: *Partisanship:* Yes, you know which side you are on, what you advocate and who you support. So be it. You point your *scepter* as you will, leaving all others equally free to choose for themselves with equal fervor. Let serendipity work for you!

Abstract: *Training:* You have found your place of learning and you now can share that discipline. Use the skills you have developed and seek to develop them further. Maybe it is time for further instruction for you or perhaps you are needed to *train* others? Let serendipity work for you!

Ritualistic: *Majesty:* You too have a staff, a scepter of your own and in your high *spirit* it can become a magic wand. Are you giving off your very best and showering your world with the magic of your presence? You have a sovereign's power and *majesty* over your world. Let serendipity work for you!

Astrological: *Clue:* There is information to be had, so stay alert to it. Allow yourself to be *clued into* what is really going on. Follow Theseus' *clew* that brings one out of the labyrinth. You are finding your way. Let serendipity work for you!

Brotherhood: *Restoration:* All is renewed. Everything is being brought back to its full usefulness. There is a reestablishment happening! Point your scepter! Serendipity brings it to life!

Symbolic
3 of Diamonds: *Organization* "A square beginning to take form."

The stone mason lifted and placed the last block into place. All day he had lifted and placed and smoothed out and perfected the fit in this orderly process. One by one he had carefully and skillfully made manifest the *organization* that was needed. He took pride in his work and now he could stand back and admire the square beginning to take form. He was building the foundation for the new structure. He was building a cathedral. "He was working within a structure according to a plan."*

Superficial: *Profit:* Now it is time to reap the benefit of your efforts. Stand back and admire what you have gained or achieved. Let stability emerge in your life.

Signature: *Detection:* This is a time to discover where your own pride is most active. Where is your skill most satisfying to you? Or are you *detecting* a lack in some area that needs to be better *organized?* Let stability emerge in your life.

Abstract: *Compensation:* The laborer is worthy of his hire and you have earned the rewards so accept them graciously. Avoid any tendency to fail to maintain

* A comment made by Rusty Carnarius re: 3 Pentacles

a genuine *reciprocity* in the give and take of life. Let stability emerge in your life.

Ritualistic: *Fame:* Your expertise has been discovered and you are now recognized. Use this for the benefit of all those involved. Let stability emerge in your life.

Astrological: *Enough:* There is sufficient for whatever is needed. You can rest a bit. Stand back and admire what has been accomplished but not for too long. There is more to build. Let stability emerge in your life.

Brotherhood: *Reciprocity:* You have arrived at the place where mutual exchange is the way and it is up to you to maintain this. You know it is a matter of giving to something to the degree you wish to take from it that is the rule. But don't forget the reverse of this. Don't give more than can be *compensated* for in one way or another or you pauperize the other! Let stability emerge in your life.

Symbolic
4 of Diamonds: *Height* "A lofty mountain peak."
The mountain peak has long been a symbol of aspiration and he remembered that as he gazed out the window at the view. The mountain range was not that high, but still it rose above the valley in a majesty of nature that was both exquisitely beautiful and soothing in its steadfastness. This was a special scene for him. This childhood memory would live on in his mind forever. The mountain rose in all its majesty before him in his mind's eye, filling him with the certainty of its attainment if he would but persevere. Be encouraged!

Superficial: *Meeting:* The time is now, the *meeting* is arranged or at least it is in the works. Let the actuality of it emerge. Aspiration meets its manifestation at least in part. Be encouraged

Signature: *Candidacy:* You are in the running. Maintain your sense of certainty as to your qualifications and your abilities. Your name has been proposed. Now it is time to look to your destiny. Be encouraged.

Abstract: *Refreshment:* It is time to *refresh* that aspiration that first brought you to step foot upon this path. Renew your inspiration. Look back through your mind's eye and view your own mountain peak. Look through the window that offers you a view of your own first seeking and move again in the eagerness of that spirit. Be encouraged.

Ritualistic: *Solvency:* Here we have three things: The ability to pay all your debts and meet all your financial responsibilities. The ability to dissolve other substances and finally the ability to solve or explain. Within yourself you hold the solution. So stand firm and proud in your integrity, dissolve the power of the outer to affect you and expect and know that you have within you the solution to any problem! The certainty of the mountain is being manifest. Be encouraged!

Astrological: *Revival:* Bring the eagerness of spirit of the original aspiration back to full vitality. Come back to life with all your aspiration intact and your eagerness now becomes an "unhurried eagerness of spirit." Be encouraged!

Brotherhood: *Readiness:* Be in a state of readiness. The time is about to come. All is in place and it is time to be prepared in every way. Check out your requisites and settle yourself for the event. Be prepared -- it is time. The view of the mountain is now crystal clear. Be encouraged!

Symbolic
5 of Diamonds: *Equality* "Settling sands."

She stood back and examined the scale. It was still not quite level. Very gently she added a few more grains of sand to the balance beam. Once again she stood back and observed and sure enough -- the scales were equal! A perfect balance was now achieved. Steadiness was manifest and *equilibrium* established. The time has come. The answer becomes available.

Superficial: *Success:* There is a satisfactory outcome here. The scale is reading well for you. The time is now!

Signature: *Settlement:* It is time to *settle* up. The verdict is in. Make the payment or collect what is due. The time is now!

Abstract: *Breadth:* It is time to broaden out and include more. The scales were generous to you and now you can afford to include more in your life. Seek unity. The time is now!

Ritualistic: *Deserts:* You have your verdict. The scales are balanced and you have your just *deserts*. It is time to recognize this. The time is now!

Astrological: *Contact:* The time has come to make the contact. Good, bad or indifferent, it is time to know, and connection is the key. The time is now!

Brotherhood: *Agency:* An active force is now in place. The means for something to be done is now achieved. Let the instruumentality be recognized. Act for yourself or as the *agent* of another. Invisible forces may be at work. The time is now!

Symbolic

6 of Diamonds: *Wonder:* "A large diamond with the power of a lodestone."

She stared at the ring. It was very old, but the pure white fire of the stone flashed in the light, and prism-like it sent all colors sparkling as she moved her hand. She was reminded of the alchemist speaking of the lodestone and how it could attract whatever was needed or wanted. Did she have the key to cosmic gravitation in this beautiful gem? Here was the symbol and reminder of the power that resides within each one of us to attract what is wanted through the power of expectation. The diamond took the light and focused it to where it spread out in every color of the rainbow just as we have the power to aggregate the outer to our inner pattern.

Superficial: *Agreement:* To agree implies a being or going together without conflict and is the general term used in expressing an absence of inconsistencies, inequalities, unfavorable effects, etc. Thus, here we have the state of calm knowing that allows for the agreement between inner choice and outer conformity to that choice. Here is the cooperation needed.

Signature: *Prosperity:* Here is the result, the good fortune, wealth, success, etc. People with wealth consciousness settle only for the best. Here is the cooperation needed.

Abstract:	*Patronage:* Here is the support, the encouragement, the sponsorship as a result of the inner concentration of the mind.
Ritualistic:	*Vanity:* Use care with your pride. This isn't done by you alone. This is accomplished through the partnership with a higher being and the working with the larger pattern and the total oneness of the universe. Here is the cooperation needed.
Astrological:	*Comradeship:* Let yourself be in a tune with the "other," the "all" and the "spirit" within all. Here is the cooperation needed.
Brotherhood:	*Alliance:* Here is the ideal interaction between inner and outer, self and other, human and high self. Be in partnership with that higher. Work with the cosmic pattern. Here is the cooperation needed.

Symbolic
7 of Diamonds: *Camaraderie:* "A glass of sparkling wine."

A congenial group raise their glasses in salute to the happy moment and offer their congratulations. In this convivial atmosphere every cooperation is available to you. The fellowship, both visible and invisible, are close and warm in spirit. The best of humankind is manifest as *laughter* fills the air and hearts are warm with joy. Skoal!

Superficial: *Laughter:* Enjoy this time and make the most of it. You are in the midst of brightening influences. A time of happy completion.

Signature: *Trust:* You can *trust* this time to be of help and assistance. Your intuition and your associates are to be seen in that light as well. Feel this and uphold it in your heart as you open your mind to reflection. A time of expecting the completion.

Abstract: *Foreshadowing:* Your mental outlook has special skills in this supportive atmosphere, so be willing to receive the intuition's messages and tune in to the possibilities. A time to focus on the completion.

Ritualistic *Optimism:* Work in this ambiance of

high morale and upbeat ideas. You have it together, so make the most of it. A time of experiencing the completion.

Astrological: *Relief:* The necessary respite is here and you can use what is needed as it now becomes available. Use this for others as well if that is the need. A time of using the completion.

Brotherhood: *Recourse:* What is needed is now available and these outer congratulations are signature of the necessary self-sufficiency within yourself. It is time to use it! You are surrounded by the invisible fellowship. It is time to be a part of the completion!

Symbolic

8 of Diamonds: *Efficacy:* "A hammer wielded with great power."

He started his recitation, and once more Longfellow's *Village Blacksmith* came alive and charged the room. The school was small and the teacher expected the best from her students. She still encouraged memorization and recitation of the tried and true. Her young student was pleased with himself and the audience of parents proud of his success. Each one was transported by the familiar words speaking of the essence of effort dramatized by the "smithy" and his "heavy sledge." We too are reminded of the "something attempted, something done" of the poem's words and the drama of putting that "plussage sense" into our lives that can lead to adventure.

Superficial: *Wealth*: Truly you are wealthy when you toil in joy with the adventure of life a part of your everyday effort. The smithy "looks the whole world in the face, For he owes not any man." To be wealthy put "plussage" into your efforts! This card indicates that you "have it all."

Signature: *Inducement:* The teacher encouraged the boy and demanded performance. Where is your inducement? Are you accepting it or are you resenting where you are being expected to perform? Maybe there is more encouragement in this than you have seen. Can you be persuaded to put more into it?

Abstract: *Anchorage:* What is it in your life that

can be relied upon — that holds firm for all your needs? Have you not discovered that this lies within you and your willingness to allow life to be an adventure in lifting everything to that "plussage sense" through your own efforts? Security lies within. Can you be persuaded to put more into life?

Ritualistic: *Craftsmanship:* If a "plussage sense" is a part of your efforts then *craftsmanship* is sure to emerge. You too "swing your heavy sledge, with measured beat and slow, Like a sexton ringing the village bell, When the evening sun is low." Can you be persuaded to put even more into life?

Astrological: *Reinforcement:* This is what the "plussage sense" is all about, a reinforcement of your ideals, the living of them in real life on an everyday level and with the touch of practical application that is reality. It is time to check -- what is being reinforced in your life that is shareable? Can you be persuaded to put more into your life?

Brotherhood: *Guarantee:* You "have it all" and you use it well through your "plussage sense." You have the guarantee of effectiveness in your realm.

Symbolic

9 of Diamonds: *Fruitage:* "A garland of victory."

He was a tourist here in Rome, but as he walked the lava street of The Sacred Way, the memories flooded back. He was the victor, received in triumph, entering Rome in a chariot drawn by four horses and proceeding along this same Via Sacra to the Capitol. Ahead of him walked the Senators, at the head of the procession, behind them were the trumpeters, carriages bearing the spoils of war, oxen to be sacrificed and the captives in chains. Then he came, the General, crowned with his laurel, the garland of victory. The scene was so real, he knew it to be true. There was some part of him that was totally capable of this victory. As he continued on, he knew himself to be something more than he had previously seen, for now he knew he was capable of accomplishing sufficiently.

Superficial: *Entertainment:* Yes, it is now time for diversion and amusement. There has been a sufficiency achieved or it is about to be.

Signature: *Acquisition:* Yes, you have acquired sufficiently through your own efforts or you are about to do so.

Abstract: *Merit:* There is worth, value and even excellence in your performance, and this is to be recognized now and given its due. Sufficiency has been achieved or is about to be.

Ritualistic: *Enfoldment:* You need to *enfold* this

new view of yourself into your innermost self. It is time to recognize your ability and your accomplishment and give it sufficient respect. With this as a part of yourself you can then *enfold* more of the world, you can embrace more of those who need you and recognize your worth. Sufficiency has been achieved or is about to be.

Astrological: *Reestablishment:* This sense of who you really are and what you can accomplish must allow you to *reestablish* yourself in life. Having done this and having seen your worth, it is time now to stand on a new sense of capacity and accomplishment and build a whole new foundation in your life. Sufficiency has been achieved or is about to be.

Brotherhood: *Stewardship:* Having sufficiently accomplished, you now find yourself with the responsibility that this has given you. You now must be the *steward* who protects and cares for what has been conquered.

                                    Symbolic
Ten of Diamonds: *Blessing* "Sheaves of wheat."
It had been a long journey to reach this point where she could stand outside the cabin and gaze at the sheaves of wheat all gathered for the winter. There would be enough to insure grain for flour for the entire community, regardless of how long the winter. It had been touch and go so many times, the storms, the insects, illness and just plain exhaustion, but they had made it through. The long journey west was finally beginning to reap its rewards. She could begin to see how there really could be a more universal sense of values lived in this place. She could feel the reserves building both actually and potentially for all of them. The bundles of grain all harvested were symbol of so much and she smiled in quiet joy as the sun set on the scene and she turned to enter the cabin and prepare dinner.

Superficial: *Sunshine:* Yes, there are brighter days emerging now. Make the most of them. You've earned it! There are reserves established.

Signature: *Harvest:* Yes, it is time for the reaping of rewards. Enjoy the *harvest* and the knowledge that there are reserves now to be counted on.

Abstract: *Insurance:* Yes, it is good to have the reserves building for the winter and maybe even more if the mind can encompass the potential that is here being revealed.

Ritualistic:	*Culture:* Yes, look now to see what else can benefit from your culture. You have proven your abilities to bring growing things to a peak that can be *harvest*ed. Isn't there more that you can see to benefit from your abilities? Appreciate the reserves you have established.
Astrological:	*Profusion:* Yes, this is a time of abundance, and you have much to be appreciative for and your own efforts are a part of this. Can you see an even greater potential to work toward now that the reserves are established?
Brotherhood:	*Sustenance:* Yes, it is a time for full appreciation of what you have and the satisfaction that can be gained from sharing it. There is food for all, so nourish as you can. Be aware of your own sustainment and support.

Symbolic
Jack of Diamonds: *Pride* "A butterfly emerging from its chrysalis."

Fragile and struggling, the butterfly hangs almost free from its confinement in the chrysalis. The boy reaches to help and the old man stops his hand. "No," he says firmly. "Mind your own business. If you help now the butterfly will always be damaged. It must make the struggle successfully on its own." Moments pass, and then in one last huge effort the butterfly emerges free and hanging, wings downward. Gradually, the wings flatten and expand, the legs and other body parts harden, and then in that long awaited moment the glorious colors flash and it soars round the boy's head and then, dancing in the air, moves away.

Superficial: *Applicability:* Yes, act, but be sure you know that your action is appropriate and relevant to the situation. Remember, don't help emerging butterflies. Work on self may be the more *applicable* effort in a real art of living.

Signature: *Leaning:* There is inclination here -- check it out. Is it appropriate? Examine it and see if under scrutiny, the "feeling" is acceptable. It could be wonderful or it could be merely a predilection from an earlier time and no longer appropriate. Make sure it is truly your business. Pay attention. This could be important.

Abstract: *Foresight:* Ah, now you know. You've made it conscious, and the inclination has clarified in its relevance. You are forearmed and aware through your ability to use your foreseeing constructively. As the old man knew from his experience of butterflies, you too have knowledge from your own experience. Focus on your future potential.

Ritualistic: *Affection:* You are strongly *affected* by what is going on, so pay attention. It was the old man's love for the boy and for the butterfly, that prompted his actions and his teaching. Check that you, too, are fully aware and acting in everyone's best interests at this time. Make your choices out of love, even if it is to allow the struggle and not to interfere.

Astrological: *Aptness:* You've got it all worked out. Your understanding has conceived the appropriate procedure. You know how to work on your own development.

Brotherhood: *Designation:* You have the ability now to see the *design*, to work from the pattern, thus the artist emerges from the chrysalis. In this achievement there is responsibility. You have named yourself to uphold it. You have been *designated*! Do it in your "style."

Symbolic
Queen of Diamonds: *Enlargement* "A figure entering an open door."

She moved into the room with alacrity as he was waiting for her, and she knew that. Her shyness was dissipating as she saw him. He was across the room and standing aside from the majority of the group. She realized that this time he was seeing her, really seeing her. She had long waited for such a moment. She had imagined the glance of recognition and the smile of welcome, and now both were there. She continued across the room and he rose to greet her. Finally, she was free to ask, "Could you help me, please?"

Superficial: *Renewal:* Yes, it is time to start fresh. A hint is given in the idea of being willing to ask. Recognize the right person and go for it! The fresh supply is now available. Be willing to use it!

Signature: *Emotion:* Yes, strong feelings are here, so use them constructively. Let them lead you to the right person, the one who can really help, or let them allow you to recognize the person who needs you. Be willing to know!

Abstract: *Felicity:* Yes, happiness now enters your life. Welcome it and allow it to be there. Recognize it and encourage it. This is a time for producing good fortune, bliss, or apt expression in words, deeds or thoughts. Be willing to accept it and use it!

Ritualistic: *Meaning:* Yes, there is much meaning in what is going on, and it is for you to be willing to accept it. Don't fall into the trap of fear and thinking it is too good to be true. Be willing to understand what is needed.

Astrological: *Remedy:* Yes, this is a time of healing. Let it be so. The cure is now manifest. Do be willing to accept it. The correction, the relief, the healing is now available if you are willing.

Brotherhood: *Preference:* Yes, it is up to you now. It is your choice. Surely, you can accept the positive that is entering your life. Can you not see it? You are being given opportunity and priority. Be willing to make the choice.

King of Diamonds: *Solvent* "A chemist's test tube filled with clear liquid."

Symbolic

He stood there, staring at the test tube filled with clear liquid, and he rejoiced. It was done. This was the cure, and the world would be rid of a dreadful ill. The time spent had been worth it. The faith and the attention to detail had been effective. Most of all, the constant holding in consciousness that the cure was possible and would manifest had paid off. Here it was! The *solution* had been found, and the problem would be dissolved.

Superficial: *Rulership:* Remember the rule. All is consciousness. Thus it is as your mind creates that the manifestation is formed. Expectation is a powerful force and needs to be under your control. Take control of your life from within yourself. "Imagination enables the self to perform the non-performable in the depths of mind, gaining the sense of ideal doing that makes the performance possible in fact or kind in the visible realms of everyday." Marc *E. Jones*

Signature: *Adroitness:* Here is skill, both mentally and physically, as a result of the mindset and the vision of the possible. Time to use the dexterity that you have manifest.

Abstract: *Judgment:* It is your privilege to judge

how things will be. You can make the decision and move from there. Remember your expectation is all powerful, so maintain your integrity of thought and point of view. Exercise your power. Don't waffle or waver.

Ritualistic: *Indulgence:* To indulge implies a yielding to the wishes or desires of oneself or another because of a weak will or too amiable a nature. This isn't the way. To merely drift will not bring about a healing. It must be a directed consciousness with effort behind the focus to actually achieve the desired result. Use your experience.

Astrological: *Propriety:* It is important to act in accordance with what is suitable. This requires a choice be made by you as to what is your accepted standard. With the choice made, then the actions may follow in due course. Live up to your own standards!

Brotherhood: *Miracle:* Here is the final result -- the event that is beyond normal, beyond usual or ordinary expectation. Here is the remarkable -- the manifestation -- THE HEALING MIRACLE!

Sabian Symbols in Card Reading

Symbolic

Ace of Spades: *Accounting* "A trumpet upraised."
He raised the bugle to his lips. The crowd was silent. The breeze was still and even the birds were quiet. He drew in his breath, and in a moment the first full notes of that hauntingly emotional sound filled the air and struck each ear with the impact of the occasion. This was the moment she had dreaded the most. This sound, like certain fragrances, could trigger her tears with the full nostalgia of what had been. Now would come the *accounting,* and it was she who was *accountable.*

Superficial: *Death:* As with all cycles ending, there is a need to pause and take stock, but remember what is important is to know that, yes, there is a break here, but then a new beginning. Look for a new perspective to emerge for you.

Signature: *Issue:* This is defined as: "A going out, outflow, passing out, exit." So, time to let it go and get ready to move on. Look for the new perspective that is needed here.

Abstract: *Surrender:* It is time to turn it over to a higher power within yourself. Call on the larger and release it to the larger encompassment. You must move in the new perspective you have gained.

Ritualistic: *Primacy:* Having *surrendered,* you now have *primacy* over the situation.

You have put first things first, or you need to do so. Let the new perspective be in control.

Astrological: *Passion:* Here is the compelling emotion that constitutes real drive and ambition, so let it be directed constructively. Let this *ordeal* move you to something more. The new perspective can be energized now.

Brotherhood: *Ordeal*: The severe trials of our lives are the turning points that move us into new life. That new perspective is all that matters, so move to it and with it.

Symbolic

2 of Spades: *Privacy* "Yellow flowers that fade when picked."

The brightness of the yellow trumpets on the lemon lilies seemed a magnet for the sun's rays. They caught the essence of the flower's being and transformed it to an even more vibrant hue. She was, as always, caught by the sight and again, as always, wished to capture it. Her hand reached out to pick the stately blooms and then, remembering, withdrew. She knew from sad experience that these lilies fade when picked and thus were symbol of the times when it isn't for you to pick or choose. Their message was blazoned in the sunlight. A delay is advantageous.

Superficial: *Scandal:* From the Latin "scandalum" meaning cause for stumbling, temptation. Here we see the meaning of the lily. Hold up. Acting as you are inclined to do at this time could offend and lead to sorry result for you. You can't pick right now. Remember, silence is a virtue. "Be still and know."

Signature: *Setback:* There is a reversal here. Progress can't move forward at this time, so accept it and withdraw your hand. Turn to other areas of effort. "Wait, and be still until you know."

Abstract: *Bereavement:* There is a loss here, and it isn't a time to take the initiative. Time is required to come to terms with what has taken place. Give yourself that time. "Wait, and be still until you know."

Ritualistic: *Advantage:* Remember, the delay here is advantageous to you. Don't see it as a negative. "Wait, and be still until you know."

Astrological: *Temperament:* Your natural disposition matters now. If you find patience a real difficulty then this is not an easy time, but if your nature is more adaptive, then this can be a time of turning your attention to other things with profit. "Wait, and be still until you know."

Brotherhood: *Withholding:* This level puts the responsibility in your hands to hold back, keep back. Restraint is a matter of your conscious choice. Permission is not being given. It is, and should be, withheld. "Wait, and be still until you know."

Sabian Symbols in Card Reading

Symbolic

3 of Spades: *Fragrance* "Forget-me nots"

In a bittersweet moment he paused in his stroll to stare down at the tiny blue flowers with their bright yellow centers. Their *fragrance* heightened the nostalgia as he remembered, saying to her in Tennyson's words, "sweet forget-me-nots that grow for happy lovers." With a sigh he moved on, knowing this was a time for lingering in separation and that he must just wait and observe.

Superficial: *Divorce:* There is separation here, and one must accept it and do with it as best he can. Detach and let it go.

Signature: *Breakdown:* The emotional impact here is heavy, and the heart and the mind must find new ways of focusing on life. The old way didn't work well and it is breaking down, so be willing to move through it and find a new way of going. Detach and let it go.

Abstract: *Disassociation:* It's time to sever the connection. Separate and understand that there is no longer any relevancy here. Detach and let it go.

Ritualistic: *Poignancy:* The fragrance triggers all the other senses, and the memories are strong. A very moving moment is involved here, and it may well evoke compassion, but still it is necessary to detach and let it go.

Astrological: *Petulance:* Don't let the little things get you down. They trigger the memories. You find yourself more irritable, but this is no help. Shift and move on. Detach and let it go.

Brotherhood: *Presence:* Bring yourself to the now. Don't live in the past or the future for that matter. Practice the presence which means seeing the beauty and the love that exists right where you are now! Detach and let go of all negativity.

Symbolic

4 of Spades: *Germination* "A child holding an egg."

He stopped, knowing something wasn't right. He was only two years old and in happy mimicry of grandmother's daily trip to the hen-house to gather eggs, here he was. He had successfully navigated the steps, coming in by dropping to all fours, but now, faced with the return trip down, something told him he had a problem. In one hand he clutched the warm, brown egg he had found in the nest the cackling hen had vacated. Nothing would persuade him to give that up. Yet how was he to climb down the steps? As grandmother rushed to the rescue, she smiled in enjoyment at the *germination,* the growing, adventuresome effort of the boy.

Superficial: *Illness:* *Ill* can mean wicked, bad, even hungry, but, in the main it is causing or tending to cause harm. The term illness can be taken in its broadest sense to mean "promising harm." So this is a time to use care and to go carefully as per the wee one with the egg. He paused, knowing to continue could be a problem and thus allowed himself to be rescued. This card on this level advises you to emulate the boy; pause and be absolutely willing to go either way -- whatever is best.

Signature: *Exhaustion:* The little guy was no doubt ready for a nap after his adventure and let this be a good object lesson for you. It's time to rest. You have gone as far as you can go for now. Ease back and stay poised for change.

Abstract: *Disattunement:* You are out of harmony in some way. Relax and rest. Let things come back into alignment. Don't hold rigidly to your course at this time. It could be the wrong approach. Stay poised for change.

Ritualistic: *Vacation:* Now that's a great idea. The boy was on vacation at his grandmother's and rescue was available to him. Maybe you, too, need a respite and a safe place to *germinate* for a bit as you stay poised for change.

Astrological: *Doggedness:* The boy was not going to give up the egg and you are not to give up on whatever it is that is your precious adventure, but it is time to perhaps see a new way of going for it! So stay poised for change.

Brotherhood: *Clairvoyance:* As grandmother appeared out of the blue for the boy, your answers may well be coming to you from places unseen. Stay receptive and open to new views, and remember that it is your job to hold the mold that is the form you wish to manifest. Hold on to your egg and stay poised for change.

Symbolic

5 of Spades: *Repercussion* "Two doors hinged so that to open one closes the other."

!The wind was really blowing, and she was glad she was so close to home. She had left all the windows open, and this northeaster was going to turn to rain at any moment. Head down, she hurried up the steps to the front door, and, key in hand, she turned the lock and pushed the door open. As she did, the *repercussion* from the shift of air inside the house slammed the open door to the bedroom with a crash. "Oh, darn," she thought, "I know better than to do that. I know I have to go easy when the wind is up this way! I know to push things under these conditions will only make problems."

Superficial: *Danger:* There is a definite dilemma here. Stay alert for false psychic impressions. All advisement is to wait, not to take any action whatsoever. Wait and see if there is further reaction to be dealt with. Stay put and wait until the danger is passed.

Signature: *Failure:* Having done it badly all one can do is learn from the mistake. Remember, to do something well it is almost always necessary to do it badly first! So, now it is time to wait and see what the reaction is that must be faced.

Abstract: *Misjudgment:* One way or another, the mistake was made. Try to see how to avert it the next time. Don't wallow in this. Everyone makes mistakes. What matters is how many times you pick yourself up, not how many times you fall down! Get up and face whatever the reaction is and don't hold animosity.

Ritualistic: *Degradation:* There is definitely a lowering of status here, but that doesn't mean you are defeated. You may have to make up for this to move ahead, but you are not finished, unless you decide that is to be. Wait and deal with the reaction without animosity.

Astrological: *Ignorance:* A healthy ego learns to admit when it doesn't know. This is your opportunity to rise to that status. There's no shame in not knowing if you are willing to find out. Realize this and wait to deal with the reaction without animosity.

Brotherhood: *Sonship:* Here is the mosaic in terms of the individual tiles involved. It is time to work on yourself, to polish up your tile. The whole is deficient until you are able to manifest your small part of it as beautifully as you have seen it to be in the whole picture. Don't push! Work with the larger and unified whole.

Symbolic

6 of Spades: *Speed* "Dolphins at play."

Smooth and sleek the six dolphins cut through the water in the streamlined effectiveness of who they are and what they are and where they are. The water is their element. Totally at ease they move at top *speed* effortlessly, for in their abandon they are totally themselves and being alive is akin to play. The effort is being expended but in the totally self-mobilized manner of a child lost in the fascination of a game. The "unhurried eagerness of spirit" that is true self-mobilization and effective *speed* which is not haste. Make life a game and rise to the challenge of it! Be in the flow.

Superficial *Enemy:* Anything less than the above and you are your own worst enemy! Stay alert for anything that holds you back from this proper action and realize it is alien to who you truly are and thus enable yourself to disengage from its influence. *Speed* is of the essence here, as described above, so mobilize to the challenge that exists.

Signature: *Prejudice:* There may be old feelings hanging around that get in the way of your eagerness to "play the game." Examine these to see if you are truly acting in your own best interests. If you can't eliminate them as obstacles, then turn to another area of activity in which you can move swiftly and eagerly. Don't dwell on the negative — Move onward. Mobilize.

Abstract: *Repetition:* Seems like you've heard this tune before, so perhaps you haven't followed the previous advice and examined this "feeling." There's a syndrome going on here, and the *repetition* is calling your attention to it. Stop, look and listen and break the cycle. It's time to understand what is causing this so you can move on.

Ritualistic: *Voyage:* Smooth sailing! The way is clear, and you are in the flow of it all. Effort is needed, but harnessed and effective as with the dolphins at play. Mobilize.

Astrological: *Abnormality:* It's normal to adapt to the demands and conform to whatever is popular at the moment. Your way is different, unique, original and creative. Because of this, be willing to be the "loner", using your creativity and maintaining your effectiveness. Mobilize to your own potentials.

Brotherhood: *Overshadowing:* Your effort has brought you to a place where your skills are refined to serve a higher expression of yourself. Watch and catch the *overshadowing* in order to cooperate and become more effective in this way. This is not dictation. It is expanded awareness.

Symbolic

7 of Spades: *Illumination* "A flash of lightning."
It is night and he stumbles as he makes his way through the blackness, thinking, "I shall never make it home. I cannot see to find the path. I wander lost and helpless in this forest!" In fear and helplessness he drops to the ground. He knows that the cold will envelop him if he doesn't keep on, but he seems unable to move. Out of the vastness of the blackness comes a brilliant flash of lightning. The sheer brilliance of the light illuminates the path and his home is within his sight!

Superficial: *Tears:* Before the lightning flash you are in sadness and the tears do come. This is a time to remember the story and it will be there. Don't give up! Turn your face to the light wherever it emerges. Seek it. Turn away from fear!

Signature: *Fear:* The emotional side can be overpowering here and the negative can loom large. It is time to work toward the light. Expect the light. This means use your disciplines to assist you to a better state of mind (and feeling). Use your affirmations and healing techniques. A memorized ritual can serve you very well in these moments. Turn away from the fear!

Abstract: *Abashment:* You may very well be taken aback for a moment when the *illumination* comes. Just be sure you look to the path and don't close your eyes to what has been given you! Turn away from the fear!

Ritualistic: *Inadequacy:* The old habits may be very strong and it is possible to ignore the new view and even refuse to struggle on after having seen the light. Break free of these old habits and make the final effort to reach your goal. Turn away from the fear!

Astrological: *Suspicion:* Not to trust the new insight is equally possible. Even having seen the way, it can be rejected if the old ways of thinking have set you up to reject it. Use your knowledge of the higher to allow you to move ahead and free you from doubt. Turn away from fear!

Brotherhood: *Fatherhood:* Know you are never alone. The "father of all, in all" is always there and thus the completeness that is the larger and the way home. Move to your ways and means for defining this and for touching the unity of mankind. Turn away from fear!

Symbolic

Eight of Spades: *Impregnation: "A spearhead pointed upwards."*

The chela was quiet, not meditating, more in deep contemplation of what his guru had been teaching him earlier in the day. The tiny, bearded man had been explaining how to even be interested in hearing negative things about others or self, let alone to actually engage in gossip of any kind, was literally to become involved in that particular karma. He had ended the talk speaking of how the mind was to be always focused on the highest, the best and the most beautiful that could be found in any environment and that in this way one kept one's karma moving upward. As he remembered, he saw there ahead of him the new frond rising from the center of a palm tree, like a spearhead pointed upwards.

Superficial: Excitement: Let this be the *excitement* generated by the good and the beautiful and never any insidious interest in anything less than that. Get high on beauty, joy, creative effort and love! Karma upward only.

Signature: *Revolt:* Rise up against the negative! Turn away from it and refuse to allow yourself to be there or to have any part in it! Karma upward only.

Abstract: *Reconstruction:* If you have found yourself imbued with the less than the beautiful and have slipped into a more fearful and antagonistic way, then now is the time for a *reconstruction* process. Rewrite your mental pictures, alter your self-talk, and emerge in an entirely new scenario. Realign karma upwards!

Ritualistic: *Arrest:* As above, it isn't necessary to continue in an unwanted direction, even mentally. Refuse to be a part of a conversation or a thought process that is not your chosen reality. You can stop it! It can be *arrested.* Refuse all but karma upward!

Astrological: *Devilishness:* "Get thee behind me Satan" is another way of saying, "I refuse to be in this place in consciousness, I will not associate with the prince of darkness. I will recognize the trap and slam the door and move ahead in the way of karma upward!"

Brotherhood: *Orders:* We can all recognize higher instruction, whatever the source, and gain from its advisement. But the actual acting upon the ideas is the relevance. We must be "good soldiers" and perform as our higher self instructs and even orders! Karma means act, andtr56g 21 only with the doing of it does karma move upward.

Nine of Spades:

Symbolic
Insulation: "Gates shut and barred."

The house was truly very grand. Imposing in its European styling, it was very like a famous German manor house, positioned high on the hill. The drive was gated, and it was here that she paused, for as those gates closed behind her this last time, she knew it meant she could not go back. There is no way to go now except forward. The old must be relinquished. It has nurtured all that is, and now it is time to leave that security and move out on her own. With a sigh of acceptance she drove through the gates and out onto the thoroughfare.

Superficial: *Stupidity:* It would be very *stupid* to try and hold on to what is over. There is no chance of maintaining things as they have been. The gates are closed now and barred.

Signature: *Stubbornness:* If your tendency is to hold fast to what has been in a *stubborn* manner, you may well make things more difficult for yourself. Hang on to what is yours, but move ahead.

Abstract: *Misarrange:* Move ahead. Something may have failed to reach its potential, but it cannot be repaired. It is a fact, and it is time to move on.

Ritualistic: *Despair:* It may feel hopeless to give up what has been for so long, but *despair* not and gather your courage. Move to the new way.

Astrological: *Vampirization:* To stay would be a *vampirization.* To allow someone else to continue in this manner in your environment is equally vaporizing, so insist that the gates be closed and barred. It is not healthy to continue in this manner.

Brotherhood: *Intuition:* It is time to know, even without reasoning. The cutting edge of what is relevant requires you to be able to *intuit* the new and thus be enabled to act in that mode.

Symbolic

Ten of Spades: *Alchemy:* The philosopher's stone. The *alchemist* patiently instructed his young apprentice. He explained that the philosopher's stone is an ancient symbol of the perfected and regenerated human being. He then added, "as the rough diamond is dull and lifeless when first removed from the black carbon, so the spiritual nature of man initially shows little luster. It is as the soul of man is ground and polished that its shapeless form is transformed into a scintillating gem from whose facets pour streams of varicolored fire." The apprentice thought, and then asked, "How can we know we actually are refining a philosopher's stone in our own personal lives?" "By our increasing disinterest in things that are of no value, and our continuing eagerness to center the self within itself as a laya center for the invisible fellowship" was the alchemist's reply. Then he added, "You must journey on through, my son."

Superficial: *Journey:* You too must "*journey* on through," so all advisement is to take hold of your situation and move it forward as is needed.

Signature: *Revolution:* You move through the cycles of your life in a patterned *revolution* through the seasons, but what you do with them is up to you. That is your free will. You may, if you find it needed, activate a total *revolution,* a complete change in your way of life. *Journey* on through.

Abstract: *Negotiation:* Yes, this effort is not unlike negotiating your way through a complicated course, and it is an adventure termed "being on the path." *Journey* on through.

Ritualistic: *Annihilation:* Yes, in the process of "the increasing disinterest in things that are of no value" there is a dropping away of these and they are in that way *annihilated* but always replaced with a new and shining facet of the diamond. Journey on through.

Astrological: *Thrill:* Yes, there is and should be an excitement with this *journey.* Your life becomes an adventure and a challenge rather than a chore and a defeat. Journey on through.

Brotherhood: *Ordination:* Originally, "to put in order," so it is time to do that. Get your life together and under control and directed toward your highest aspirations. You can decree or order this for yourself and "journey on through."

Jack of Spades: *Insignia:* "A spray of joyous colors."

Symbolic

Thinking about it, I suppose this card is really the epitome of the symbols. When Dr. Jones wrote of Zoe Wells obtaining the fifty-two symbols for the deck of cards, he said that when they ended the session, an ancient seal was described by Miss Wells as a mode of certification for what had been put down, but no record was made,, and later attempts to reproduce it were uncertain. "However, this was the beginning of a conscious recognition of the ancient sources as a self-contained and living integrity available for use." When I was beginning this project, a seal was given to me. Is it the same one? I have no way of knowing, but when this card is involved it is high indication of that living integrity that is available for our use. {The seal is shown at the end of the Prologue.}

Superficial: *Effort:* The using of effort to get something done. You may be embarking upon a project as I was. You may not have seen it as yet, or perhaps you have just finished one, but, either way, it needs to be given its due as it is of some importance to you and no doubt to others. Be ready to cooperate.

Signature: *Eagerness:* You are anxious to do, to be "up and at 'em" and this is good. Be enthusiastic and move ahead with the work that is to be done. Be ready to cooperate.

Abstract:	*Possibility:* Think of what is *possible, what may be accomplished or achieved and live in that possibility!* Be ready to cooperate.
Ritualistic:	*Chivalry:* This term evokes all of the values of the age of *chivalry* with its knights and ladies. This is a time for courage, honor and a readiness to help. Follow your cause. Be ready to cooperate.
Astrological:	*Action:* Yes, it is time to act, to be busy about what is truly your work, your dedication, your cause in life, your mission. Be ready to cooperate.
Brotherhood:	*Ceremony:* You may wish to seal this effort with a ceremony of dedication, an indication of the high integrity involved and your touch with the sources behind it. Whatever is going on needs a formal and courteous procedure. This is not to be taken lightly. Something of import is taking place, so be ready to cooperate.

Queen of Spades: *Reserve*   Symbolic   "A well neither as dry nor as dark as it seems."

The sun's heat is unmerciful as she drags one foot after the other, weaker with every step. The terrain is dry, and she ran out of water some time back. Her strength is ebbing, and her only hope is the well. Will it be dry as sometimes happens this time of year or will it offer her the needed thirst-quenching water? At first glance it appears abandoned and waterless, but on closer examination it is not as dry nor as dark as it seemed. You have unused potential at your hand, so be willing to use it.

Superficial: *Resurgence:* This is a time of refueling and a coming back to life. You are revived! Water is always a symbol of completeness, the oneness of life. Thus you can draw on the larger group consciousness in this process. Be willing to go on.

Signature: *Abandon:* It is always darkest before the dawn. Don't quit now! The waters of life are so close. Things are not so dark as they seem. Don't give up!

Abstract: *Remorse:* If the temptation to give up is allowed to overwhelm you, it will lead to regret. So, don't settle for remorse. You can make it. You may have given up in the past and now you live with the *remorse* — let that experience teach you to "hang in there." Be willing to keep on trying. Ask for help. Be willing to cooperate.

Ritualistic: *Heartache:* The racial consciousness holds a powerful negative sadness here, so it is necessary to override the drift and know that you can move beyond the past and the "negative" pull. Keep going, knowing that the well is not dry no matter how many say it is or how many times it has been in the past! Your experience can be different now! Cooperate with the positive flow.

Astrological: *Dissipation:* Don't settle for self-indulgence and old habits of a less than worthy kind. Just because you have never made the "big push" doesn't mean you can't -- go for the gold this time! Remember this card indicates an unused potential. Ask for help and be willing to cooperate.

Brotherhood: *Teaching (and thus learning):* Having held on to your center and made the supreme effort, you now know how. You have learned and thus you can be an example and dramatize the teaching. Realize you will learn even more from the teaching role. Be willing to learn, regardless of your age or situation. There is still a further untapped potential to be developed. Work within the group consciousness and be willing to cooperate.

Symbolic

King of Spades: *Tenacity* "A slow-growing sapling of great strength."

As he wandered through the forest, he was in awe of the age of these trees and the strength they personified. As he looked up they seemed to reach to the very sky with their greenery far above his head, communing with realms he could not touch except through them. He walked on and came upon a younger tree, a sapling no doubt in the realm of redwoods, but still a large tree by human standards. He leaned against it and felt the surging growth move through his body and the strength of the support system it offered him. He was strengthened, and he realized he, too, was capable of being a slow-growing sapling of great strength! He could lean on all the strength of the past, and through its aid he could direct his life to heights beyond his personal limitations.

Superficial: *Might:* You have a great or superior strength, power, force and vigor to work with at this time, so contact it and use it. You are complete, effective and possessed of power so long as you know you are a part of something so much more than just yourself. "Stand on the shoulders of the giants."

Signature: *Perspicacity:* You can now gain a broader view, a new perspective, so allow it to emerge and encourage its sources that are at work in your life. "Stand on the shoulders of the giants."

Abstract: *Poise:* You move now with dignity and equilibrium. Use this dignity of manner that your self-assurance allows you, for you are now truly more than you know. "Stand on the shoulders of the giants."

Ritualistic: *Lordship*: You are indicated as having the power, so use it wisely. Especially use care not to merely *lord* it over anyone out of personal ego. "Stand on the shoulders of the giants."

Astrological: *Advocacy:* You must know what it is you truly support and wish to *advocate* in the world for you now have the opportunity to be the spokesman for something more than just yourself! "Stand on the shoulders of the giants."

Brotherhood: *Hierarchy:* You are a part of or in touch with a spiritual *hierarchy* of significance or you could be, so pay close attention to what is required of you. This is important and your behavior must be in every way equal to the responsibility inherent in this card, for this is the most powerful card of all. "Stand on the shoulders of the giants.

Sabian Symbols in Card Reading

Symbolic

Ace of Hearts *Metamorphosis* "A ripened nut opening of its own accord."

The stately hickory nut tree was golden in the autumn sunlight, and at long last the first hard, round gift had fallen to the ground. The husk opens in four sections to reveal the inner nut, now fully mature. The alert, little chipmunk watches with excitement. It is time to pay attention. It is time to know and to begin — at least within yourself.

Superficial: *Opening:* See it and be aware. Something is giving you a signal to begin. The fruitful phase of the cycle has begun. Reap your rewards, move through, and let the insight in. Be prepared to think in new ways and consider new possibilities. If you stay focused, you are bound to reach your goal.

Signature: *Proposition:* There is a proposal in the air. Do you feel it? What are the possibilities here? Do be willing to hear it out, feel it out, and consider the new potential. If you stay focused, you are bound to reach your goal.

Abstract: *Pregnancy:* The new cycle has just started. It is still developing subjectively and the birth of the living form is still in the future. You are nurturing a whole new possibility.

Surely, if you stay focused, you will reach your goal.

Ritualistic: *Purification:* The old is no longer germane as there is now a new and pure emergence. This is unsullied and emerging clean and unencumbered. Clean up in preparation for the new, for if you stay focused, you will reach your goal.

Astrological:: *Reverie:* This is a time for contemplation and meditation as you seek to identify the profoundly significant transformation that is taking place within you. Pause and ponder on the potentials opening up for you. Avoid merely day-dreaming, for it is as you stay focused that you reach your goal.

Brotherhood: *Message:* With the opening of certain centers you are now able to receive the long-awaited *message* from a larger and broader level of consciousness. Pay attention and allow the *message* to emerge. The fourfold is now functioning, and you may bring valuable information into consciousness. Be sure you are willing to give it full attention as you focus and move toward your goal.

Symbolic

Two of Hearts *Emancipation* "A file and sundered iron bars."

Smiling, he walked through the *opening* (*Ace♥*). He was free! Once again he had the advantage, for his captors had no idea of his long, hard effort with the file, night after night. They never came near this back area of the building until evening, so he knew he was safe to move quickly to the rear door and make his escape. With any luck they wouldn't discover him gone for many hours yet, and he could be successfully finding those compatriots of his who would support his efforts.

Superficial: *Festivity:* Yes! It is time to celebrate and greet one another in joy and the spirit of the festival. Hold on to your advantage!

Signature: *Satisfaction:* Yes! Take *satisfaction* in it for you have earned it. The complete fulfillment of your relationship needs can be here now. You have left the restriction and the limited way. Hold on to your advantage!

Abstract: *Happiness:* Yes! Go ahead. Enjoy the feelings of pleasure and contentment that are yours now. Hold on to your advantage!

Ritualistic: *Climax:* Yes! You have reached the summit because this is the culminating event in the series. You have arrived so make the most of it. Hold on to your advantage!

Astrological: *Evidence:* Yes! The proof is now here and the facts become obvious and they are all in your favor. Hold on to your advantage!

Brotherhood: *Relevancy:* Yes! What is happening now really is as important to your life as it appears to be and it is a positive! Pay attention and realize it is significant, and hold on to your advantage!

Symbolic

Three of Hearts *Vigor* "A harnessed waterfall."
The sunlight sparkled on the flume's waters as they rushed to the turning wheel. With a splash the buckets, each in turn, were filled and moved on quickly as the next bucket was close behind. The wheel continued to turn with rhythmic cycling and the energy was harnessed to run the mill. The process was so exquisite to watch, in its simplicity and high effectiveness. The two men turned from admiring their handiwork to shake hands in full appreciation of having used well the genius of the other.

Superficial: *Marriage:* A true partnership is possible now. The harmony of the wheel and the water demonstrates the potential. The cooperation of the two men who built it is an even more apt illustration of the mode of operandi that is required and available with this card. Remember to make full use of the genius of the other.

Signature: *Warmth:* There is heat here, and heat is energy, so use it. The warmth of feeling can be applied in constructive ways to accomplish what is needed and desired. You can share as you make full use of the genius of the other.

Abstract: *Elaboration:* What is being addressed here is worked out carefully with much effort and it needs this kind of attention. The painstaking attention of the two men who built the wheel is now an illustration of the process

Sabian Symbols in Card Reading

involved and the potential satisfaction ahead. Make full use of the genius of the other.

Ritualistic: *Proclivity:* Watch your inclinations. The water in the flume flows to a constructive use, so be sure your efforts are equally well directed as you make full use of the genius of the other.

Astrological: *Contribution:* As in the *marriage* between the two builders, it is possible to use the genius of the other constructively now. Allow this kind of interaction to make its *contribution*, one to the other and then to all as with the energy produced by the wheel.

Brotherhood: *Insemination:* There is an influx of ideas and these are the waters that will turn the wheel if you have built that well and are prepared. They may be the beginning conception of the wheel itself (whatever yours may be). The way now leads you to accepting the genius of your own conceptions. Remember that the genius of the other's insights can be wonderfully helpful. Seek advisement if you need it. Or your special expertise could be exactly what some other needs. Encouragement can be insemination.

Symbolic

Four of Hearts: *Royalty:* "A golden girdle."

It had been a short life and a desperately sad and unrewarding one. Now, in intimate review of this with his mentor, he listens intently. He is being given to understand that he is "always" of royal blood and the keys to achieving immortality are focus, and interest in something that sets you on fire with passion for it. "Find something you love to do and work yourself to death at it."* Limitations dissipate into the ethers when you transcend time and space by losing yourself in something you truly enjoy.

Superficial: *Surprise:* Here is the sudden, unexpected break-through. As in the above scenario, this can be in insight or it can as well be your recognition and *surprise* as circumstances are cooperating with you. Whatever, be *loyal* to your inner sources of strength and guidance. Don't settle for too little.

Signature: *Adherence:* As above, it is important to maintain a real touch with your own *royalty* within and not allow your self-image to be diminished. Live up to the best of yourself as you remain loyal to your inner sources of strength and guidance. Don't settle for too little.

Abstract: *Contentment:* You must be at peace with yourself, and this can only be if you respect yourself. Respect for personality begins with self and then can expand to include all others. To love others, you must love yourself and to love yourself, you must know yourself to be worthy of love. Thus you can be content with yourself even as you stretch to be even more of what you can be. Remain loyal to your inner sources of strength and guidance. Don't settle for too little.

Ritualistic: *Haven:* There are many safe places in the world but none are guaranteed. The outer support is always subject to shift and change. Real security can only come from within. Don't settle for too little.

Astrological: *Concentration:* Defined as: "To increase the strength, density, or intensity of." Here is what the boy had lost touch with. He failed only in that he didn't *concentrate* his attention on that "golden girdle within" which holds the touch with the All. Be loyal to your inner sources of strength and guidance. Don't settle for too little.

Brotherhood: *Progress:* To move forward is inevitable if you maintain a touch with that golden place within in which everything that ever was and ever will be is available to you. There is no need to settle for too little.

* Marc Edmund Jones

Symbolic

Five of Hearts *Melody:* "A street musician playing."

The sound could be heard some time ahead of the presence and the cheery mood advanced ahead of his steps. The children came from everywhere as to a magnet and the hurdy-gurdy rolled along in a throng of laughter and smiles. The small rhesus monkey strutted among them with his tin cup outstretched to catch the many coins. He doffed his tiny, red cap in appreciation of every one. The little, old man turned the crank with renewed *energy* with every smile as he knew there was no issue here, just the joy in the now which was his very life.

Superficial: *Victory:* Truly you are victorious as you can realize the joy and beauty of life itself that is found in the true reason for your being, your chosen effort.

Signature: *Backbone:* Here is the renewed *energy* to turn the crank of life and move ahead as it is achieved from within yourself. You stand taller and prouder in your integrity of self. Here you start to live your chosen effort.

Abstract: *Energy:* Fill yourself with the renewed *energy* found in the living of life from this *victorious* perspective.

Ritualistic: *Vogue:* Laughter and joy are contagious and dissolve negative issues. Can you start a trend? Could this way of life not become the "in *vogue"* style. Aren't you the trend setter? If not, why not?

Astrological: *Conception:* Is this idea not born within you, and is it not now your conviction? Are you not pregnant with the *concept* of living your life this way? Is a concept not an idea at work?

Brotherhood: *Immolation:* Here is the creative self-immolation of the mind and heart at work in the way of joy. This is the giving of the self to something more. Lose yourself in service, as the gift of the spirit that the burning up of the self up in a chosen creative work can be.

Six of Hearts: *Exclusion* Symbolic "Two hands raised in diffidence."

That evening she had been doing her prayers but not in bed as was her usual rule. She was standing, getting ready for bed, and as she sought spirit, there was a knowing, a recognition of a presence in the room. Her mind said, "I am seeking spirit so this can only be a beneficent being," but her feelings said "No, this isn't good." As the presence became stronger and closer, she knew this was not of spirit. Immediately, she rejected the presence and moved to the healing ritual, and with that, whatever it was dissipated and was gone. There are some things in every life in which there is just no need to be involved. There can be invisible aid when one is unable to handle it himself.

Superficial: *Concession:* Defined as to grant or cede. There are times when there is just no need to become involved and when the responsibility is to be turned over to another, visible or invisible.

Signature: *Whim:* Use care with the idle and passing notions, capricious ideas or desires. A sudden fancy that moves you out of your established way of going can be an invitation to the less than desirable within yourself and without. This applies to both visible and invisible. No need here to become involved.

Abstract: *Liquidity:* The psychic realms are so fluid, they are without form and thus able to masquerade, pretend. There is no need here to become involved.

Ritualistic:	*Opinion:* You have a right to your particular judgment. In fact, it is your obligation to yourself to know what that is. Thus, if something doesn't feel right to you or doesn't seem right to your mind, then it is your right to act on that until proven wrong or you find a new perspective on the situation. There is no need to become involved here.
Astrological:	*Encompassment:* We each have our own environment, territory and space. It is ours to respect and protect and do with as we will. It is necessary to encircle the good and the beautiful and the best of all that is at hand. It is your choice as to what you include and how you do so. Keep your sights on your desired achievement and include only what takes you there. Avoid the traps of the side trips that have no real relevance for you. No need to become involved.
Brotherhood:	*Secret:* The Esoteric side. There might be an inner group involved here. The disciples of your mystery school may be at hand It is important to know when, as now, there is no need for *you* to become involved as you can then leave this to the invisible to handle.

Sabian Symbols in Card Reading
Symbolic

7 Hearts: *Reawakening* "An hour glass inverted."
The wizard slowly lifted the hour glass and examined it. The green marble base at each end pleased him as did the symmetry of the fine glass globes held to the bases with bright brass rods. "Yes," he thought," this is truly a fine symbol of time." He turned the glass over and placed it on the ancient wood surface. "The sands are just starting to run" he thought. There is all the time and chance that's needed!

Superficial: *Nourishment:* You are in the midst of everything that sustains and nurtures you, so it is time to move ahead and make the most of this. Use this time and allow a new cycle to emerge. There is all the time and the chance that is needed.

Signature: *Inevitability:* Having found the support you need, it is time to feel the surety within you of the new insight. There is all the time and the chance that is needed.

Abstract: *Welcome:* Greet the new phases with a real *Welcome*. Recognize that they react to you in the same manner. It is time to respond in kind to the positive greetings as there is all the time and the chance that is needed.

Ritualistic: *Endowment:* The time has come to

accept your heritage as it has been given to you. Take a moment here in which to appreciate your support system and the strength of your roots. Even the wizard may be readily at hand if needed. Remember there is all the time and the chance that is needed.

Astrological: *Consolidation:* It is time to incorporate, merge, unite! You've come a long way, and you can now be more effective in a combined mode, so pull things together and let it be more streamlined. Remember, there is all the time and the chance that is needed.

Brotherhood: *Resource:* Time is your greatest commodity and asset. Use it well and make it work for you. In this manner you may well become a resource for more wonderful things as you remember you have all the time and the chance that is needed.

Symbolic

8 of Hearts: *Ambivalence* "A good and evil angel standing together silently."

The white and silvery one stands facing the sunlight, and it illuminates and showers her with golden rays. The dark and shadowy one stands to the side as if waiting. The dark angel waits for a moment of slippage, a touch of fear, or a sadness that overpowers the light. So reestablish yourself in the light and allow no slippage to interfere. Remember, everything that ever was and ever will be is here right now, and you must choose to stand in the light!

Superficial: *Dream:* Hold to the positive and the vision of that bright and wonderful world that you aspire to achieve. Identify with the white and silvery angel and stand in the sun! You must choose your dream!

Signature: *Liberty:* You are free, free to do as you wish. and you must know that! Feel it and stay in the *dream* as described above. Feel the bright and silvery angel's presence in your life. You must choose your dream!

Abstract: *Facility:* The bright angel offers you insight into your *dream* and how to achieve it. You must choose your dream!

Ritualistic: *Outreaching:* The bright angel offers

you ways and means that move you toward your *dream* -- reach out for it. "There is no taking without the reaching out to take"* Don't hesitate, for that gives the shadowy one power. You must choose!

Astrological: *Genius:* Know your own creative strength and ability, and use it. You are standing with the bright one, and the sun illuminates your *genius*. Allow it to emerge into the light! Use your talent to achieve your *dream* as you hold to your choice.

Brotherhood: Reassignment: You have been here before, but maybe you don't remember or maybe you do. This is a second chance. Reach out for the new way and allow your assignment in this world to manifest. We come to earth with sealed orders! The bright angel is offering you the envelope to read at this time. The *dream* becomes an *assignment* as you hold to the choice you know is of the light.

*Omar's Quatrains by Marc E. Jones, Page 13

Symbolic

9 of Hearts: *Fullness* "The shimmering sea bathed in the setting sunlight."

They sat together quietly on the deserted beach. Only the sounds of the sea in its surging forward to the shore and its movement back to the vastness of itself were to be heard. The talkative gulls were silent. The entire scene was held in the glow of the sun as it made its descent to the water. In this celebration of the day and its accomplishments, the golden orb was king indeed. The brilliant color spread across the sky, the sea, and the beach. They, too, were bathed in this gold as they basked in knowing that their desire was granted, their wish come true, their will achieved.

Superficial: *Wish:* Dare to move toward and achieve what it is you want. This card is affirmation of consummation. Don't waste the wonder of this time. Be about your business in your own behalf and let it happen! Remember, this is the wish card!

Signature: *Gain:* Add to yourself those things you desire. The time is right for expansion and realization. Let the timing work for you as you seek and find. Remember, this is the wish card!

Abstract: *Repletion:* It is accomplished. It is yours. You are *replete.* Now it is time for appreciation and sharing. Let the *fullness* of it all serve you and yours well. Remember, this is the wish card!

Ritualistic: *Maturity:* Enough has been accomplished now that you can recognize your own maturity. You are no longer the inexperienced one without success. You know now the ways and means of the process and the "feel" of success as well as failure. Remember, this is the wish card!

Astrological: *Salvation:* You are saved! Rescue is at hand! Harm is now averted and difficulty thwarted. This can even be the religious experience of being rescued from the consequences of error. You are redeemed. Remember, this is the wish card!

Brotherhood: *Recommittal:* It is time to start again: to renew your vows, to rededicate yourself to your highest aspiration and highest good. Let this be a new beginning of real worth. For Sabian students this may be the recommittal of signing in at Full Moon. Remember, this is the wish card!

Symbolic

Ten of Hearts: *Position* "A double garment."

He realized the lined garment had long been a symbol of quality, and he appreciated the workmanship in this gift she had created for him. The wool was soft as only cashmere can be and the color warm as sunlight. He knew how many petals she must have gathered for this strength of hue to emerge in the threads. The inner side was as elegant as the outer, and, as he felt it settle over his shoulders, it became the mantle of authority she had known it would be. He was now dressed fittingly for all eventualities.

Superficial: *Glory:* You are most certainly dressed fittingly for any occasion. The *glory* is yours. You have won the honor and the admiration. You have reason to be proud.

Signature: *Repute:* Consider your *reputation* as it is important at this time. The estimation of the group as to what you are reputed to be *is* of significance. Don't risk it foolishly in any lack of integrity and thus not be dressed fittingly for the occasion.

Abstract: *Shelter:* Protect your assets on all levels. Be conscious and focused on providing the necessary *shelter* for you and yours. This may be physically, financially, emotionally or mentally. Your *position* requires this sense of responsibility on your part if you are to be dressed fittingly for the occasion.

Ritualistic: *Importance:* There is an *importance* connected with what is taking place with and/or around you. Don't take it too lightly. Be willing to accept the influence that your *position* holds and dress fittingly in all ways for the occasion.

Astrological: *Conclusion:* There is an *important* last step involved here. This may be in a mental *conclusion* that you are formulating or even an emotional issue. Whatever it is, it needs to be done with awareness because it has a definite closure connected with it. You need to be dressed fittingly for the occasion.

Brotherhood: *Faithfulness:* Well, you've gained the *Glory,* the *Position,* and the *Reputation.* Your ability to *Shelter* all of this has an *Importance* to more than just yourself. The *Conclusion* will depend upon your *Faithfulness.* This *Position* demands the rhythm and order that is the quintessence of the *Faithfulness* that allows you to be dressed fittingly for all occasions.

Symbolic

Jack of Hearts: *Subjugation* "A cloaked figure entering a cave."

The wizard moved across the sands to the cave entrance quickly with his cloak swirling out from his shoulders, bell like, as he merged in and out of the shadows. Once within the sheltering walls of stone, he lit the candles on either side of the sacred place and settled in to perform the ritual. He had come here for this purpose: to bring the issue under control, to direct consciousness to a higher level of values, and, to generate the magical, healing energy.

Superficial: *Creation:* Something is coming into manifestation. Stay in control and be sure it is something of a chosen nature. Focus your art, skill, inventive imagination, in short, your consciousness to *create* what it is you wish to be your reality.

Signature: *Comprehension:* That higher level of consciousness that the wizard was tapping with the ritual is the level of greater inclusion. This is the need here; include and understand. Take in more, allow it to enter, and strive to experience the knowing.

Abstract: *Concord:* Be there in the harmony of it, the friendly and peaceful relations. Exist in consonance.

Ritualistic: *Task:* This is the task: to raise the consciousness, to dramatize the higher and the significant in life. Let this be the focus of attention as with the wizard.

Astrological: *Cognition:* Now *comprehension* has achieved *cognition!* The knowing! The process of knowing is now active. Your perception, memory, judgment, etc. are all contributing to your conception. An idea may well be born at this time.

Brotherhood: *Patience:* Here you are endowed with *patience* or asked to exercise it and further develop it. The steadiness, endurance or perseverance in performing the *task is the issue now.* Here is the calmness and the self-control of the wizard in action. *Patience* is the dramatization of *cognition.*

Symbolic

Queen of Hearts: *Residue* "The kernel of a peach stone."

As he held the sun-warmed fruit in his hands, he delighted in the range of peach-toned shades that it displayed. He was enjoying the many colors named after it. Finally, he broke it open at that magical built-in division line and, as sometimes happens, the pit split. Fruit -- it's immortality so-to-speak. This revealed the inner essence of the fruit, *residing* there unprotected. He smiled his *approval* as he saw the process of life displayed for him in this one moment captured in his hand.

Superficial: *Pliability:* The peach yielded to the man's touch and opened itself up to life. You, too, can be equally *approving* of the pressures upon you to manifest your full potential.

Signature: Remembrance: Stand on the shoulders of giants that have gone before and enhance this depth of yourself through remembering that they are there. You can call upon their help and wisdom when needed and their *approval* when deserved.

Abstract: *Complacency:* Be leery of merely relaxing and drifting. It can be smugness. Be sure it is the true self-satisfaction that comes from a job well done. Be willing to reach the depth within you that only comes from mobilizing to meet the pressures of life. Strive only for that higher level of *approval* that has real relevance.

Ritualistic: *Prophecy:* If you are truly in touch with the depths of your wisdom then it is possible to prophesy because history does repeat itself. Be willing to use this skill to allow you to stay on track and involved in the more effective effort. Use your experience and realize where the *approval* is deserved.

Astrological: *Impressionability:* Here is the ability to be impressed upon, a necessary skill if one is to be enabled to contact the wisdom of the past and the giants. Be willing to allow the capability for being influenced in this way to manifest itself through your intellect and emotions. Do not take instruction unless it is asked for and only in the areas requested. Remember, you must *approve* the value of the *impression* or negate it.

Brotherhood: *Approval:* Now we perceive the skill achieved and the depth reached and the usefulness of your impressionability established. You have a "go" from mission control.

Symbolic

King of Hearts: *Restitution:* "A couch of pure white flowers."

The meadow was covered with white daisies in full bloom. As she strolled up the little rise, they blew against her legs in the soft breeze. The walk was longer than she had remembered, and with the sun warming her chilly body, she found herself getting drowsy. She looked around at the expanse of white flowers, and it was an invitation to stretch out, which she did. Her mind drifted back to earlier years and the game of finding cloud pictures. Her eyes searched the heavens as she rested on her couch of pure white flowers, and her body restored itself.

Superficial: *Reasonableness:* Signs may be found anywhere, clouds included and the ability to reason includes the ability to draw inferences from signatures.

Signature: *Standing:* The woman stopped and stood there and appraised the situation and *reasoned* it was time to rest. Your *standing* in your situation allows you to survey the situation and decide, what next?

Abstract: *Graciousness:* The world is a friendly universe and gracious to those who find it so. Be there and accept the kindness, courtesy and compassion. Then reciprocate.

Ritualistic: *Archetype:* It could be that the heavens were the original model and thus the archetype for all else. Day or night, the patterns exist. Do we have the eyes to see?

Astrological: *Psychology:* It is time to think of the mind and its processes. How do you use it? Can you recognize the patterns and the cycles? Astrology could be helpful.

Brotherhood: *Retrospection:* It is time to stop and review that which has taken place. There is nothing so valuable as your own experience, but its value is most often found in review. Do you recognize what you have gleaned from this? Have you seen what you might have done and thus can do better when next given the same opportunity?

Ace of Clubs: *Amusement:* "A child skipping rope"
Symbolic

She is about eight years old, leggy and thin, having just sprouted up a bit. The jump rope flying about her, she smiles as she skips her way home, accompanied by the revolutions of the rope. Her dress is out-grown, and her shoes scuffed. The jump rope is nothing more than a frayed and worn out length of clothes-line, but the enjoyment is real and fresh and new! The smile is of delight as she *amuses* herself and never even sees the deprivation that surrounds her. She is making life a game!

Superficial: *News:* Something is coming into existence that you have never been aware of before. Watch for the mailman, the special delivery, the e-mail, the pictures in the clouds and the whispers in the wind! Make it a game!

Signature: *Modification:* A slight change may make all the difference. This can be in the way you are looking at things or in a practical application. Remember, an old, worn out clothes-line can become a new and wonderful toy! Make it a game!

Abstract: *Liberation:* Set yourself free! There is nothing that can jail your mind. Remember, you choose the perspective you hold on life and events. Make it work for you! *Amuse* yourself by devising ways and means to eliminate restriction from your life. Make it a game!

Ritualistic: *Vitality:* Live! Call on your *vital* energy and come alive! Yours is the power of endurance and survival. Yours is the physical and mental vigor. You are the living symbol of whatever you choose to be. Have you chosen? Why not? Make it a game!

Astrological: *Response:* Don't just react to the *news*. Direct your *response* in a chosen act! How best to do this? Play with the possibilities involved! Volunteer for what you prefer to do instead of just accepting what is offered to you.

Brotherhood: *Place:* This is your domain, your geographical locale, your position in that milieu, your situation in consciousness. Something is taking *place* or coming into existence. Are you in tune with it? Are you alert to the signals? Pay attention to the centers of consciousness, the different *places* in your body that pick up signals. Are you playing the game?

Symbolic

Two of Clubs: *Privilege*: "A royal crown"

A great teacher was speaking, and she slipped in quietly and sat down. The audience was totally under his spell, completely caught up in his words. He was speaking of the symbol of the crown. Smiling, he said "There is one thing about a crown. If you are wearing one, you have to stand up straight or it will fall off!" This is important because each one of us needs to walk with respect for ourselves and stand tall in the full knowledge of our uniqueness. We are seeking a more spiritual consciousness. The body is our vehicle for doing this. Thus it is our *privilege* to dramatize the best that we are in every way. When this is done, we tend to be accepted as "special" and treated as VIP's. Act it and you are recognized as being that. So go ahead, stand tall, even if it is a case of "fake it 'til you make it!"

Superficial: *Obstacle:* Relationships aren't aligned correctly here. They aren't forming around the best that you can be, so it is necessary to put up an *obstacle* to protect yourself from the unwanted. Build a defense! You aren't ready!

Signature: *Discouragement:* It is difficult to not succumb to *discouragement* occasionally, but that is not helpful. It is within your power to alter this mood and attitude. All is consciousness and it is important that you change your mood. At the moment you aren't ready.

Abstract: *Loneliness:* This may be the most difficult of all moods to eliminate. There is such a poignancy in our yearning to share our lives, but it is time to know you are never alone and that you are surrounded with love and light. At the moment you aren't ready.

Ritualistic: *Mischief:* As mentioned under Superficial, it is necessary to protect yourself from what is undesired here, and you are in a situation where there can be *mischief* of one kind or another going on. As the relationships are not aligned correctly, do close the door on this, for you aren't ready.

Astrological: *Vacillation:* As our will weakens and we slip to our lower centers, then weakness emerges and our high resolutions and aspirations can be subject to *vacillation*. The energy is drawn away from who you truly are, back to the "less than what you can be" mode. Firm up your convictions and remember what you are all about and how special you are. Don't accept less! Give yourself time on this. At the moment you aren't ready.

Brotherhood: *Incompleteness:* Don't give up! You are not done yet! You haven't seen the whole story or accomplished everything you can do, so don't throw in the towel! You may not be ready right now, but you are not done yet!

Symbolic

Three of Clubs: *Undercurrent:* "A field of moonflowers"

The night air was soft and fragrant with the scent of the moonflowers. She stopped to admire the pure white blooms as they stretched across the field. The moonlight seemed to linger on their trumpet-like petals and find itself mirrored in their whiteness. She felt the psychic energy that was manifest in this like an *undercurrent* flowing just beneath the surface. Something was sharing its sentimental contribution, allowing it to linger on even as it meets with its dissolution.

Superficial: *Loss:* It is time to let go of something. Allow it to dissolve. It may be something you wish to lose! Maybe it is as simple as selling it and allowing another to find use for what you no longer require. The sentimental attachment can linger on without the actual ownership. Let it go.

Signature: *Disillusionment:* Sometimes we fall into *disillusionment* before we can let go. Strive to realize that whatever it is, you have attracted it into your life for a reason. There is no value in bitterness. There is something to be gained from this experience. Find that and let the rest go.

Abstract: *Rupture:* In some instances the "letting go" becomes an actual breaking apart or a bursting from within the self. Whatever, it is still the necessary relinquishing of something that is no longer needed and must be seen as such. Sometimes breaking free is explosive. Let it go.

Ritualistic: *Shrinkage:* Yes, you are now reduced in some way. This can be seen as an asset or a deficiency. It is up to you. Either way, you must let it go.

Astrological: *Depletion:* It is time to let the inventory run down. There is no need to carry such an overhead or overload. Allow this to happen in constructive ways so it will not be necessary that it become a forced situation. Let it go.

Brotherhood: *Seership:* Here is the ability to lose the limited view of the single ego and thus see into the broader perspective. The true prophet emerges as you let go of the personal perspective.

Symbolic

4 of Clubs: *Adornment* "A fan and the promise of a scarf."

The maid handed her the fan and she turned to receive the scarf over her shoulders. Nothing happened. The scarf was nowhere to be found. In haste, she went through the door, her words hanging in the air behind her. "Do hurry and find it and bring it to me downstairs!" She ran out the door to the party, thinking, "Drat that girl, I wonder if she will find it?

Superficial: *Worry:* Here is the tendency to focus on the negative possibilities and all advisement is to "Have no fear!"

Signature: *Assumption:* Don't jump to conclusions here. The verdict is still to be announced. Stay positive and expect the best. Check your communications and practice precise speech. Have no fear!

Abstract: *Harassment:* Don't "bug" anyone about it and don't allow yourself to be so used. This is a time for positive expectations and no focusing on the negative. Have no fear!

Ritualistic: *Uneasiness:* Nagging negativity is about, so stay clear. Pay attention to what you can do, but don't allow a waste of energy in "What if?" Watch out for "the sky is falling" syndrome.

Have no fear!

Astrological: *Waste:* There can be a real *waste* of time and/or energy here unless you stay focused and move ahead with productive thought and action. If one thing is in abeyance, you can turn to another effort and accomplish much while you are waiting. Have no fear!

Brotherhood: *Impression:* Do pay attention to your intuition in controlled and disciplined skill. There can be a productive use of your divinatory skills here. Again, keep in mind the need to "have no fear!"

Symbolic

5 of Clubs: *Temerity* "An open boat safe on an uncharted ocean."

The boy was young and a novice sailor, so with his whole being commanding him to stay calm, he listened while his father explained. They had most foolishly come out in an open boat and now, having survived the onslaught of the gale from one direction, it was only a matter of time before the other side of the storm would strike. They were safe on an uncharted ocean but only for a time. They were in the eye of the hurricane. The father knew what to expect, and he felt there was a possible solution to their dilemma. He explained to the boy that if they worked together and did everything possible during this time of hiatus, then possibly it would be enough to get them through. With frightened eyes, the lad rose, saying, "What shall I do first?"

Superficial: *Jealousy:* There must be absolute *jealousy* in respect to this time. It is necessary to be very watchful or careful in guarding or keeping your situation under control. Do not allow it to be stolen away by the elements involved. Protect your own interests.

Signature: *Uncertainty:* There are no guarantees here. You must work diligently and hard to prepare knowing only that there is a possibility of solution. Protect your own interests as best you can.

Abstract: *Helplessness:* Don't succumb to this

feeling even though there is some truth in it. A deeper level of consciousness says you have a chance. So do all you can to protect your own interests and do it now!

Ritualistic: *Scuffle:* Yes, there is apt to be a "confused hurry and bustle," but that's better than dragging your feet as you don't have a lot of time. Protect your own interests.

Astrological: *Covetousness:* Yes, you will need to want it desperately. You'll need to want the life that all are given. Do not to allow yours to be taken from you, physically, emotionally, mentally or spiritually. Others have succeeded so fight for your chance to live! Protect your own interests.

Brotherhood: *Execution:* It's time to carry out the instructions. Do it! Perform! Protect your own interests.

Six of Clubs: *Exploration* Symbolic "A shaft leading down to deep treasure."

He was an old man now, but he remembered well. He listened to the younger men around the fire talking of their hopes and dreams of striking it rich. He'd searched for gold and silver in these hills all of his life. Because of this he knew all of their emotions, their hopes, their disappointments and the sacrifice they had to make to continue the search. It was a lonely life, and he'd lived it for a lot of years. He'd made some strikes, and there was money enough. Oh, nothing like the millions he had dreamed of, but enough. The truth of it was that the search was all there was left. He had no family and few friends, but he had the search and he had learned to enjoy it. Successful or unsuccessful, he was content with what he had. His life was built on his experience, and he knew how to "get down to basics."

Superficial: *Poverty:* Yes, you need to "get down to basics" and really use what you have. Do an inventory and work within your limitations in a realistic manner.

Signature: *Delay:* Yes, some things must be *delayed* as your situation and your circumstances will not support them. Whatever is involved, turn to something else that can be accomplished at this time. Don't bemoan the fact that some things are delayed. Use what you have and "get down to basics."

Abstract: *Restriction:* There is limitation in this situation and at this time, but, remember, you are learning to "get down to basics," and you can use the experience constructively if you are willing to *restrict* your inclinations at this time.

Ritualistic: *Mendicancy:* Realize that if it is necessary to ask for help, there is no shame in this. You will recover in time and be able to repay the favor. So "get down to basics" and use what is there to be used, even assistance, if necessary.

Astrological: *Extravagance:* Here is the flip side of this situation. *Extravagance* may have been the cause of the current diminished situation, and, if so, you need to confront that error and come to terms with it constructively so it doesn't repeat. If it is not a past indiscretion, you may be heading for one. Remember: this is a time for getting "down to basics."

Brotherhood: *Becoming:* It is time to move from knowing to *becoming.* It's time to "walk your talk." "Getting down to basics" is the living of the ideals and the concepts. You no longer can be merely thinking about them or studying them — pick up the task and go to work!

Symbolic

7 of Clubs: *Equilibrium* "The dorsal fin of a fish." The freshly hatched and very small fish swam quickly for cover. The memory banks that we call instinct reminded each one to stiffen its backbone. This raised the dorsal fin that is the stabilizer and allowed them to maintain their *equilibrium*. The memory voice was there, even more effectively, when the dorsal fin was raised, for there was a greater receptivity to that "higher guidance."

Superficial: *Nervousness:* As one cycle of life closes and you need to ready yourself for embarking on the new one, there can be *nervousness*. It is a clue to the need to "stiffen the backbone" and get in touch with your own memory banks and the "higher guidance." You need the outer cooperation, so stay alert!

Signature: *Apprehension:* Pay attention! Catch that fleeting feeling that adds to your understanding. Don't let this remain as foreboding or dread. Stiffen your back bone, sit up straight, "close the diaphragm" and get in touch with your higher centers. You need the outer cooperation, so stay alert!

Abstract: *Resignation:* As the recognition of what is involved here starts to emerge and your receptivity to the higher knowing becomes clear, it may mean an acceptance and submission. This could possibly require a *resignation* from some older situation. Be sure and then accept your higher destiny with the realignment of spirit that this can bring. You need the outer cooperation, so stay alert!

Ritualistic: *Defense:* Keep your guard up. At the same time you need to be careful it isn't *defensiveness.* It can be a case of defending against the pull of the past. Keep that backbone stiffened! You need the outer to cooperate, so stay alert!

Astrological: *Timidity:* Maybe you are shy, afraid to face what is taking place. Work with this. Don't just accept it. Stiffen the backbone, close off the diaphragm and get in touch with your "higher guidance." You need the outer to cooperate, so stay alert!

Brotherhood: *Surveillance:* Time to be aware and watchful! Something is a-foo. You need to stay in touch with the higher to be alerted to what is needed. Watch your signatures. Use your divinatory tools. As is relevant on each level here, keep the backbone erect and the radar tuned in to the higher. You need the outer cooperation, so stay alert!

Symbolic

Eight of Clubs: *Commission* "A silver mounted sword at rest in a scabbard."

Deep in the forest in its scabbard of stone waits the gleaming, silver handle of the sword Excalibur. How many years has it waited? How much longer will it be before the one hand that can move it from the grip of the stone moves to accept its invitation? "Are you not ready?" asks Merlin? Have you not come to the point where you are ready to take your place in the scheme of things and fulfill your destiny? Isn't it time to sever your connections with the immediate conditioned milieu and reach for your higher obligation? All commissions are self-bestowed. Pull your sword from the stone!

Superficial: *Theft:* Something is being taken from you or you are taking something from someone else. Sometimes ineptitude holds sway or a lack of awareness or someone's carelessness can keep the message that is yours from arriving. When this card is active, there is a message you aren't receiving or recognizing. Maybe you aren't seeing something as it really is? Have you failed to recognize your Excalibur and your higher obligation.

Signature: *Divestment:* Are you overloaded with things of no real significance to you? Is it time to simplify your life? Is this a requisite before you can reach for your real *commission?* Rid yourself of the unnecessary to make room for your higher obligation?

Abstract: *Renunciation:* Have you areas in your life that are holding you back? Habits? Attitudes? It is time to cast off what is holding you back and move on to a more significant way of life and your higher obligation.

Ritualistic: *Transience:* Are you living with superficial things that will not last? It is time to take a good look and see if you are building anything lasting in your life as well as looking to see if you are making some contribution to life per se. Time to pick up your higher obligation?

Astrological: *Perversion:* Have you turned away from what it is you know you should be doing? Have you been led astray and find yourself in a situation that really isn't who you are? Turn around and move toward what is right for you and what allows you to make your contribution by being who you are in your own uniqueness. Fulfill your higher obligation.

Brotherhood: *Mission:* You have a special duty in the world. You have a special work to do. Accept your *mission* in life! Draw forth your Excalibur and with it your higher obligation!

Nine of Clubs: *Inertia* "A wooden top among a number of toys."
                    Symbolic

There in the corner of the closet was the old, wooden top with almost all its paint worn off laying totally quiescent on its side. She reached to pick it up, thinking, "My life is like this. The essence of a top is movement and action exactly as is true of a human life and what have I done with mine? All those years, and what have I to show for them? I, too, have been lying on my side, unwilling to make the effort, terrified to take the risks. Always afraid and hedging my bets rather than really believing in myself and working at it! I've been living so ineptly, but there is still time. Surely I can still do it!" With this thought, she turned and briskly left the room.

Superficial: *Lie:* Defined as: "A falsehood, to give a false impression." Here you may be living so ineptly that your life itself is a lie. It doesn't truly express the essence of your selfhood. You may be living an existence that is less than what you are capable of manifesting and sharing and contributing! Don't settle for so little! Get up and act!

Signature: *Impotence:* Defined as: "Lacking physical strength, weak, ineffective, powerless or helpless." This is the danger when this card is around. Don't settle for this powerless state. You are far more, and you can do it if you are willing to focus, and, put forth the effort, and change the old habits. Find out what is holding you down so you can get up and act.

Abstract: *Inanition:* This is a lack of strength or spirit. Exhaustion. Try to understand why. What is it that is sapping your strength and robbing you of your spirit? Is it your own fear and inability to rise to what you know you wish to do and must do? Get up and act.

Ritualistic: *Resistance:* Can you exert the needed *resistance?* Can you fight off the unwanted? The negative drift isn't who you are. You are much more than that. Put forth the effort to withstand the onslaught of the old, outworn ways that hold you back from being who you truly are. Get up and act!

Astrological: *Foolhardiness:* Careful. As you first strive to act in your own self-interest, you can be daring in a foolish way that is rash or reckless. Use care when you get up and act.

Brotherhood: *Karma:* Your fate or destiny is the sum total of your acts, so be up and about your karma. *Karma* means acting in your own behalf and manifesting your talents and developing your skills. Fulfill your full potential. Get up and act!

Ten of Clubs: *Generosity* Symbolic "A bamboo basket filled with rice."

The rice paddy was still in the late afternoon sun as she finished harvesting the area. The only sound was of her feet moving in the water against the stalks. Her bamboo basket was filled with rice. She was content. The way was provided for the coming winter. Food would be available for the entire village. The famine wouldn't overtake them, at least not in the foreseeable future. She hoisted the heavy basket to her shoulder and began the walk home to her family. All was well in her world.

Superficial: *Employment:* Use something! Go to work! Let the mechanics of the procedures involved move things ahead in a profitable manner. Hire someone if needed. Get it done!

Signature: *Assignment:* It's your job! Go to work! You have your *assignment*. Get it done.

Abstract: *Liquidation:* Clean it out! Clear it up! Get rid of it! Move it out! Get it done.

Ritualistic: *Decoration:* Make it more attractive. Fix it up. Let the *decor* reflect the occasion. Or maybe it is you who is to be *decorated* because you did get it done!

Astrological: *Adventure:* Excitement reigns, and your way is one of wonder, but the need is still there. Rise to the challenge and have an *adventure*. Get it done.

Brotherhood: *Commitment:* You agreed. You have promised to do it. It is a fact now. It is your job to get it done.

Jack of Clubs: Symbolic
Source "An ancient sacrificial altar in the open air."

She had never understood the role of Abraham in the Bible. The Rabbi had stressed the importance of this ancient Hebrew's contribution. She read again Genesis: Chapter 22, the story of the sacrifice and the conversation between Abraham and God. Now the Rabbi's words became clearer. "Abraham established the potential for a truly personal relation with God." Yes! She realized, "He conversed with God! He was a partner with God! He was not a puppet but a partner!" We each must work with the higher, all-encompassing pattern, but that higher needs the individual to manifest it. Our immolation is to that higher, and our cooperation with it needs to be done consciously.

Superficial: *Interest:* Defined as: "A right or claim to something, a share or participation in something." Yes, claim that right and work with that *Interest* from that *Source.*

Signature: *Sincerity:* "*Sincere* implies an absence of deceit, pretense, or hypocrisy and an adherence to the simple, unembellished truth." This is what is required to maintain the contact and the cooperation as a partner with God.

Abstract: *Longing:* Within us all is that yearning, that strong desire. You may never have recognized what it is you *long* for. You may have thought it was various things at different times. It can be confused with possessions, lovers, drugs, alcohol, food, the green grass on the other side of the street. In actuality it is always this touch with and partnership with *Source*.

Ritualistic: *Flight:* Defined as: "An outburst or soaring above the ordinary" or "to run away, flee." Let it be the former.

Astrological: *Stimulation:* A synonym here is animate, which means to bring life to something, to make spirited. Here is vivacity and a brisk, lively quality of life. Let spirit *stimulate* and bring you truly alive!

Brotherhood: *Medium:* Become a good *medium* for conducting spirit. Abraham listened to God. He was able to hear God because of his *Interest* and *Sincerity*. His *Longing* was focused on the ideal pattern, the higher consciousness of spirit, and, the wholeness of life. He was face to face with and truly a partner with God. He could communicate with that higher level of consciousness. So can you!

Queen of Clubs: *Offering*   Symbolic   "A child with a basket of flowers"

Smiling, she skipped along the garden path. Having been given permission to cut the flowers, she was now finished, and her basket overflowed with blooms. This was a dream come true, to have the garden as her own, to cut whatever she chose and to fill the basket. Now came even greater joy. She would visit each of those with whom she shared so much and *offer* each the blossom of her love.

Superficial: *Vibrancy:* Let yourself be as *vibrant* as the child. There is a living, throbbing life here, a vigorous, energetic livingness that comes of putting more into life. Make your efforts an offering of your very best blooms.

Signature: *Payment:* Give forth those gifts your efforts make possible and offer these in *payment* for the many gifts you have received. Make *payment* joyfully. Receive it the same way.

Abstract: *Hesitancy:* This is too good to be true? You can't believe you are set free in the garden to choose among the blooms? "He who *hesitates* is lost" is an old adage, but it now applies.

Ritualistic: *Pledge:* Ah, there is a promise

involved here. Are you living up to it? Have you made it? Is there an *offer* out there waiting for your promise? Are you pledged to something or someone, and are you not making the most of that? In Robert Herrick's words, "Gather ye rosebuds while ye may."

Astrological: *Quiescence:* "Be still and know that love is here. Be still and know that wealth is here. Be still and know that peace is here. Be still and know that hope is here."

Brotherhood: *Coincidence:* There is a convergence here, so do pay attention! Are you being offered a blossom? Have you one that is needed or wanted? Look to the moment to *offer* you what is needed or wanted.

Sabian Symbols in Card Reading

Symbolic

King of Clubs: *Recollection* "A gossamer veil that fades before any direct gaze"

The spiritualist minister spoke of the veil between the dimensions. The psychiatrist spoke of the thin veil between the conscious and the subconscious, and now the new physicist speaks of the shifting of a person's consciousness from one level of the hologram of reality to another. Are these not merely different languages for expressing the same experience? It is necessary to speak in the language of the country in which you are traveling, especially when speaking of the things that the gossamer veil can reveal. Always remember that it is never revealed to any direct gaze.

Superficial: *Politics:* It is time to exercise the smoothly gracious social manner of one who deals with people easily and tactfully. Speak the language of your associates. Have the sensitivity to recognize what that is. Can you allow the veil between you to fade?

Signature: *Recapitulation:* A synonym here is palingenesis which is defined as: "Birth over again; regeneration. The doctrine of successive rebirths. The repetition of the evolutionary history that takes place in utero." Go back over. Do you have *recollection*? Can you allow the veil to fade?

Abstract: *Instinct:* Defined as: "The inborn

tendencies to act in certain ways of the species." Here is the presence of the past and its spontaneous outreaching through you. Let it work constructively through you. Allow the veil to fade.

Ritualistic: *Legacy:* Here is everything that has been handed down to you by your ancestors. The veil is very thin between now and the past. Are you in touch? Can you use the legacy in its positive best? Allow the veil to fade.

Astrological: *Phantoms:* Are the figures from the past that surround us in myth, in legend, in poetry and fiction constructive in your life? Have you the sensitivity to allow the ancestral line to contribute to you effectively? Can you allow the wisdom of the elders no longer with us, to contribute to your effectiveness? Allow the veil to fade.

Brotherhood: *Authorship:* Can you be the author of something? Can you use the wisdom of the past in your act, deed or writings and thus become the creator, the *origin*ator of a new landmark, however small? Allow the veil to fade.

EPILOGUE

You have come to the end of this little book. I sincerely hope your journey has been both enjoyable and stimulating. If it has brought you more in touch with your aspirations and your higher self, then I've succeeded wonderfully well. If you've enjoyed it and feel you have gained some insight, then that, too, is a happy message for me. If you are intending to continue your use of the book and its ideas and perhaps achieve a high degree of mastery of this skill, then I'm cheering you on every minute of the way!

If achieving a high degree of mastery is even in part expressing your hopes then I have a suggestion. This is the idea of your developing a scrapbook or a journal that is your experience of the cards. Choose a notebook. Perhaps loose leaf is the best so that you can add and delete at will. Divide this into sections, one each for each of the cards. With this ready, it is a matter of clipping the pictures and lines of text that you perceive as you go about your daily life that illustrate your understanding of the various cards. For example, if a photo in some periodical of a wonderful sunset finds you recalling the significance of the 9 of Hearts on the Symbolic level, then do clip that photo and paste it in this newly developing notebook. A line of text shouts to you in terms of "Do it!" and you know you just have to put that in with the Brotherhood meaning of the 5 of Clubs. Whatever takes your attention this way, inquire of yourself,

"What does this mean to me?" With your answer comes the message that can be included in your new journal in notebook form. This becomes a scrapbook of the tarot ideas that speak to you.

Then, as this book develops, you have your personal reference source when reading a layout is confusing you and a card asks to be understood in depth. The notes and illustrations you have included from your experience in this notebook will serve you well and offer you additional and very especially necessary input for your understanding of your layouts.

Make your personal notes in this journal as well. If a card reminds you of a certain person in a layout, then note that under that card in your notebook so that later, when questioning that card, you will be reminded. It is amazing how quickly we can forget our insights unless we do something to make them permanently accessible to us. When a card has a special meaning of any kind, note that in your collection of personal insights that is developing in this scrapbook. These are the most significant meanings of all, for these are the means of your making this skill your very own.

My final words are "Have fun with this!" We are here together in this game of life, and, even with its challenges, it is to be enjoyed!
        MAKE IT AN ADVENTURE!

Delle Fowler

Sabian Symbols in Card Reading

DATE: TIME:

QUESTION: LEVEL:

THE CUT CARD IS AND SAYS TO REMEMBER:

                                              COMBINED
RED: BLACK: KEYNOTE: OVERVIEW

THE PAST IS A MATTER OF:

09 - THE UNDERSTANDING IS INVOLVED WITH:

10 - THAT WHICH IS IN CONTROL IS:

11 - REACH FOR:

12 - THE SUPPORT IS IN THE:
SUMMARY:

THE NOWNESS IS:

01 - FOCUS ON:

02 - VIA:

03 - DON'T OVERLOOK AND STAY SENSITIVE TO:

04 - YOUR STRENGTH IS IN THE:
SUMMARY:

AHEAD LIES:

05 - START WITH:

06 - MAKE AN EFFORT TO:

07 - THE GREATER OPPORTUNITY IS IN:

08 - VIA:
SUMMARY:

| CONCLUSIONS ARE: |

The Four Worlds confirm and add:			
The World of Self	The World of Responsibility	The World of Relationship	The World of Spirit
09	10	11	12
01	02	03	08
05	04	07	04